Swedish
Child Massage

In this book Lena Jelvéus takes us step by step through the growing years of life showing how touch from the heart is as necessary as food and air. She teaches how and when to touch through a simple yet thorough massage, touching games, and fairytales. This book is a wonderful handbook for new mothers, fathers, aunts, uncles, and teachers. I recommend it as a must have to all involved with our most precious resource–our children.

Maria Grove
Founding Director of Touch Therapy Institute,
Encino, California

Swedish Child Massage

A Family Guide To Nurturing Touch

BY LENA JELVÉUS

SWEDISH HEALTH INSTITUTE®
Your Source for Health & Wellness

Swedish Child Massage

A Family Guide To Nurturing Touch

By Lena Jelvéus

Photographs: Anders Jelvéus

© 2004 Swedish Health Institute ®

Disclaimer

The content of this book has been reviewed and checked for accuracy by a medical doctor, massage teachers and massage therapists. However, author, editor and reviewers disclaim all responsibility arising from any errors that might occur as a result of the inappropriate application of any of the information contained in this book. Child massage is not a substitute for appropriate medical and pediatric care. If you have questions about the appropriateness or application of the methods described in this book, consult a pediatric health care professional.

Printed in Canada

ISBN:0-9718124-0-3

Content

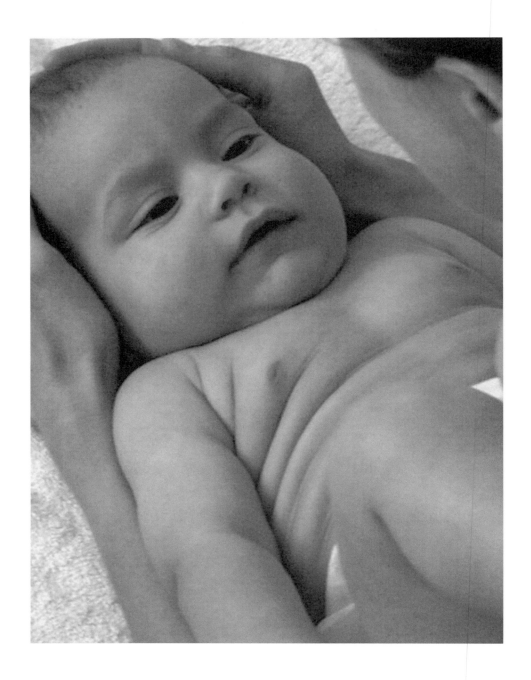

Preface

Life is a gift as well as a wondrous journey. Along this journey we all want to be as healthy and happy as possible. We put our gifts to good use to the best of our ability. Hopefully we find things along the road to make us feel good and to heighten the quality of life.

To me, touch has been of vital importance to physical and mental well being. As I have grown, matured and learned, I have come to the insight and understanding that the need for touch is something I share with all other beings on earth. There are physiological systems in the body that are directly related to touch. These have to be stimulated to maintain our wellness and in some cases even our survival.

This book is about the largest organ of the body – the skin. It is also about hands. The common denominator is touch, and what touching of the skin does to the growing child.

Much of what I intend to share may seem obvious, and if so, that is fine. However, I hope to deepen your understanding of touching, as well as to shed light upon and to inspire you to an increased awareness of what you can do and achieve with your hands.

Touch can be anything from a gentle stroke to a firm handshake, or a peaceful hand on the shoulder, to an effective massage. Every contact between people where skin meets skin, or otherwise body contact is made, is included in what I refer to as touch. In most cases, touch, massage, and tactile stimulation, are interchangeable. The important thing is that the intent, regardless of how the touch is performed, is well meant and loving. If touch is to have the positive effect I am claiming in this book, the heart must be behind it.

In the following chapters, the importance of touch will be described more thoroughly in relation to the different stages in childhood. Most of what is presented is based on clinical and scientific studies spiced up with my own experience, as well as with that of friends and colleagues. To make it as easy to read as possible, the sources are not quoted in the text but are listed in the bibliography.

Lena Jelvéus

Introduction

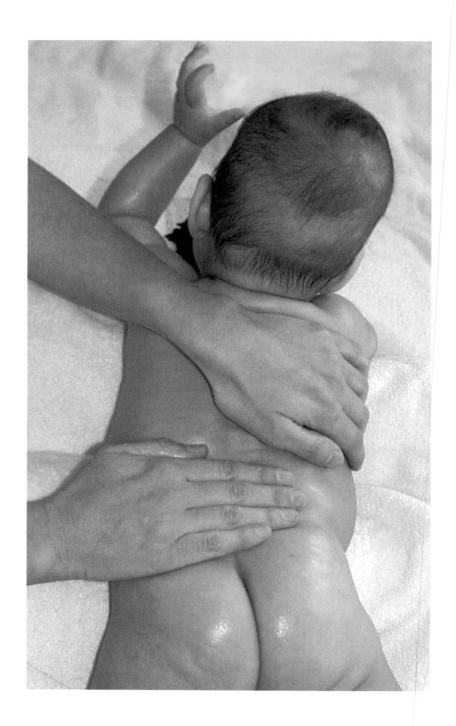

The use of hands,

as a tool

to show friendship,

to comfort and heal the ill,

to express love and tenderness,

to calm and stimulate the child,

is as old as life itself.

Bernard Gunther

We are born with a hunger for air, food, and touch. If we breathe, air enters our lungs; if we eat, food enters our stomachs. But how do we satisfy the hunger for touch? As helpless babies we are cared for by caring hands that touch us. We are rocked, bathed, and clothed. Through the care given by our parents, our hunger for touch is more or less appeased. Some of us receive an adequate amount of touch, while others live with a constant need for more. The need is deep and sometimes the touch is not substantial enough. The characteristics signaling an inadequate fulfillment of touch have not always been recognized since the condition is expressed in various ways. However, past and present generations continue to find external and varying solutions to the problems caused by the lack of touch.

The need for air, food and touch remain. Though we continue to breathe and eat, we go through childhood, adolescence and into adult life with expressed or unexpressed wishes for closeness and touch. Each and every one experiences life's doses of heartaches, separations, successes, misfortunes, and physical ailments. Little do we know how our experiences of touch effect our readiness for such challenges or how it aids us in our capabilities to deal with them. It is quite typical that when the body and soul are aching we then seek help. This in itself may lead to a first contact with massage as a tactile method appreciated for how it fills the need for touch, and for the other tangible positive effects massage has on both body and soul.

The march of massage into America

In the past, massage has frequently been associated with luxury and flair. Massage has been looked upon as something that the person of leisure could fill their time with, but it has not been readily recognized as accessible to the working class. Unfortunately massage has also had a stamp of misgivings and has been associated with less serious activities. Today however, more and more people are acquainting themselves with massage and other kinds of bodywork and therapies. Existing massage schools have been working on elevating the status for massage technicians and massage therapists, and at the same time increasing the level of information and education to the public about the positive effects massage has on the human being.

The Swedish gymnast Per Henrik Ling is considered the father of Swedish Massage. It was not an easy task however, to introduce massage to society, not even to the Swedish, where there were doubters then as there are now. When Ling, in 1812, asked for permission from the Swedish government to teach massage, he was given the answer that: "There are already enough tightrope dancers and riding acrobats." It was not until a year later, after having healed a prominent and influential person, that the decision was re-evaluated. Ling was a pioneer and inspired people from all over the world, including Americans, and soon therapeutic massage started spreading.

The fact that massage is good for keeping in shape has been known for centuries. The Roman gladiators were massaged before they entered the arena to better manage their challengers.

In a book for medical doctors published in 1925, Henrik Berg, M.D. and doctor of Philosophy (1858-1936), wrote the following:

" The art of giving massage is of such an ancient lineage that it is lost in the night of history. In Finland the "thumb ladies" have long been known for their skills. [...] In Sweden massage gained a good reputation when the crown prince of the time, under the conduction of the Dutch doctor Metzger, recovered after massage treatments. Massage has since then been the object for scientific studies, and many doctors have made the same their specialty. [...]

Execution. – It is totally useless trying to learn the art of massage through only reading. The theory is acquired from good teachers and from books. The practical part is added, and that is the most important part, as it is when learning how to play the piano. – There are many different kinds of massage that can partly be divided into the type of strokes used–stroking, kneading, tapping etc., and partly typed after the organs that are treated. [...] Coconut oil is a very good substance to be rubbed on the skin in massage, widely superior to Vaseline.

Effect. – Massage is a superior method to promote absorption of extravasation and old inflammatory exudes, to dissipate ache, fight stiffness and rigidity and to, in general, increase the nerve and life activity in some organs. There are also cases when massage must not be given. To these belong tumors caused by cancer, sarcoma and tuberculosis, abscesses, scrofulous lymph nodes, acute illnesses and in particular inflammations, which appear suddenly e.g. in the stomach or lower abdomen. It is totally wrong to want to "give massage" as soon as one feels a lump.

Use . – The number of ailments that can be treated with massage, are almost unlimited. Here, some ailments may be mentioned: headache, migraine, facial ache, sciatic pain, cramps, hysteria, emaciation, muscle atrophy (common after fractures, as a result of bandaging and surgical dressing), polio, nose catarrhs, (outer and inner nose massage), chronic stomach and intestinal catarrh, stomach enlargement, constipation, diseases of the lower abdomen, general nutritional disturbances such as anemia [...]; also nerve weakness, ailments in muscles, tendons and joints, muscle rheumatism, muscle strains, chronic rheumatoid arthritis, gout, eye diseases, and lastly at deliveries.

A skilful masseur usually combines massage with gymnastic treatments. It is too bad good massage treatments are expensive. If it were cheaper more people would every day let them selves be massaged. In Japan and China it is the specialty of the blind to give massage. Without doubt massage will develop further and win a large and blessed following. There are few remedies, which are considered natural that areas effective and harmless correctly given as massage. The human hand is after all the loveliest of tools.[…]"

Massage has, over the years, risen and fallen in popularity. At the turning of the millennium we can again see an increasing demand. It is not only among the adult population that massage has become an accepted method of healing and well being, but even the young and the elderly are receiving the message about touch. Even though traditional massage has existed in our culture for quite some time, it is the southern, exotic countries, that have inspired the custom of massaging babies. One would think it is the most obvious thing in the world that the little ones be sufficiently held, hugged, and massaged. Children usually enjoy more touching than the grown ups do. But in my opinion we are in many ways too parsimonious with the tactile sharing with both old and young.

The "non-tactile" society

In today's society many still have a built-in misunderstanding about touch. We live in a "non-tactile" society and therefore we usually have very little experience of being touched by our fellow beings. Research has revealed how tactile communication differs from one country or culture to another. In one study it was registered how many times a couple sitting in a cafe touched each other. In Puerto Rico the people touched the most, 180 times in one hour. The Americans brushed against each other twice in the same length of time. In Paris people touched 110 times, and in London not at all.

For those who have grown up in a "non-tactile" society it might seem suspicious, and even unpleasant, if someone they do not know touches them. Many also react negatively if they are touched by mistake. We are truly far from the behavior our cousins the monkeys have. They touch and pluck each other all the time. It is interesting to note that this behavior seems to stabilize both the individual monkeys, as it does the whole crowd.

There seems to be a certain difference in how men and women experience touch. It has been observed that women touch others more frequently, and also receive touch more frequently than men do. Women usually experience touch positively, too. Men, on the other hand, more easily interpret touch as a form of dominance, a violation of their private space, or lack of independence. Even in situations where touch is nothing other than contact or care, there is more of a tendency by men for misunderstanding and misinterpretation. In many cases, for both men and women, touch is most appreciated if it comes from a person of the opposite sex. That is also true for touch that is clearly non-sexual. It remains so, that for the majority in our culture, frequent touching among adults is reserved for sexual partners.

The single person, without child or close friend, can live their lives in tactile poverty. Variations exist regarding how much body contact is exchanged in different situations, in one and the same culture. Factors such as family, heritage, and social class often play a determining role. For example, it is more likely that a person with a higher status touches someone of a lower status, than vice versa.

Nevertheless, to mother nature we are all equals. The need for bodily nourishment in the form of closeness and contact is more or less the same for everyone. We have now come so far in our understanding of the physiology of touch that it seems only natural to do something to soothe the suffering from the lack of touch we are experiencing in this culture. The actions that can be taken range from massage at the work place, massage in sports clubs, to massage in hospitals, schools and kindergartens. These techniques coupled with the most important of all, touching of one's own children, will not only enhance the health and well being of separate individuals, but will also support the positive development of society and influence the evolvement of the future as well as the global peace process.

"Rimerick"

A generous man that I know
Was stroking both friends and foe
So that they were agile,
Their health's no more fragile.
Massage is their medicine now.

-L.J.

The wrong kind of touch

On the subject of massage, people often turn up their noses and question what it is all about. In some people's minds, massage is associated or even equal to some form of sexual activity. It is sad to note that ignorance about massage and touch still exists, and that this healing, nurturing touch, has become confused with erotic stimulation. For the misinformed, a recommended means of obtaining the correct information is to receive a professional therapeutic massage treatment. Most misconceptions are thereafter dissolved.

When it comes to massaging children and touching minors some people get upset. We are today painfully aware of children and children's bodies being abused and exploited for pedophilic purposes. To an uninformed parent, activities such as Child Massage and School Massage may sound suspect. It may seem contradictory, but I would like to say that it is to prevent such abuse that we need massage and touch in schools and in day care. It is of great importance, however, that touching requires knowledge and skill by the performer, not only technical proficiency. A deep understanding and ability, as well as theoretical basis of touch related reactions, and the means of such, is a requirement for every professional giving a child a massage.

The greater the child's hunger for touch, the more likely it is to be swayed by somebody giving attention and blandishment while touching the wrong way. A minor, who has had rich tactile experiences, and a child who has been touched by hands full of parental love, will have a better chance of retreating when an adult is touching them with erotic intentions. This is partially because we can assume the child has a stronger sense of self and will therefore more easily dare to object, and partially because the child can more clearly feel the quality of the touch. There is, of course, no guarantee. However, I want to insist on the better odds for a child with tactile acquaintance than for the child deprived of touch and security.

It has been noted that pedophiles and child abusers often have had an emotionally rough upbringing. Tactile safety has been denied them from their early years, and most parental touching has been in a punitive manner. In the absence of any other adults to compensate for the imprudence of the parents, these people have grown up with greater or lesser behavioral disturbances. Child molestation is an expression of such a disturbance.

We cannot guarantee our children that they will escape the threat of abuse, but we can at least do everything possible to give them a safe and loving foundation, so that they, as adults, do not have the need to violate small children.

Every parent and adult dealing with children should wish to have the insight and strength to ask for help in the occurrence of sexual attraction to a child's body. It is in the nature of touching that feelings are awakened. A feeling of nurturing closeness, with the emphasis on experiences of the senses, can be accepted in the adult-child relationship. Sexuality, on the other hand, cannot.

Please Touch Me

If I am your baby, please touch me.
I need your touch in ways you may never know.
Don't just wash and diaper and feed me,
But rock me close, kiss my face and stroke my body.
Your soothing, gentle touch says security and love.

If I am your child, please touch me.
Though I may resist, even push you away,
Persist; find ways to meet my needs.
Your goodnight hug helps sweeten my dreams.
Your daytime touching tells me how you really feel.

If I am your teenager, please touch me,
Don't think because I am almost grown,
I don't need to know you still care.
I need your loving arms, I need a tender voice.
When the road gets rocky, then the child in me still needs.

If I am your friend, please touch me.
Nothing lets me know you care like a warm embrace.
A healing touch when I am depressed
Assures me I am loved,
And reassures me that I am not alone.
Yours may be the only comforting touch I get.

If I am your spouse, please touch me.
You may think that your passion is enough,
But only your arms hold back my fears.
I need your tender reassuring touch,
To remind me I am loved just because I am I.

If I am your grown-up child, please touch me.
Though I may have a family of my own to hold,
I still need mummy's and daddy's arms when I hurt.
As a parent the view is different,
I appreciate you more.

If I am your aging parent, please touch me
The way I touched you when you were very young.
Hold my hand, sit close to me, and give me strength,
And warm my tired body with your nearness.
Although my skin is worn wrinkled, it loves to be stroked.
Don't be afraid. Just touch me.

Anonymous

Touch at the beginning of life

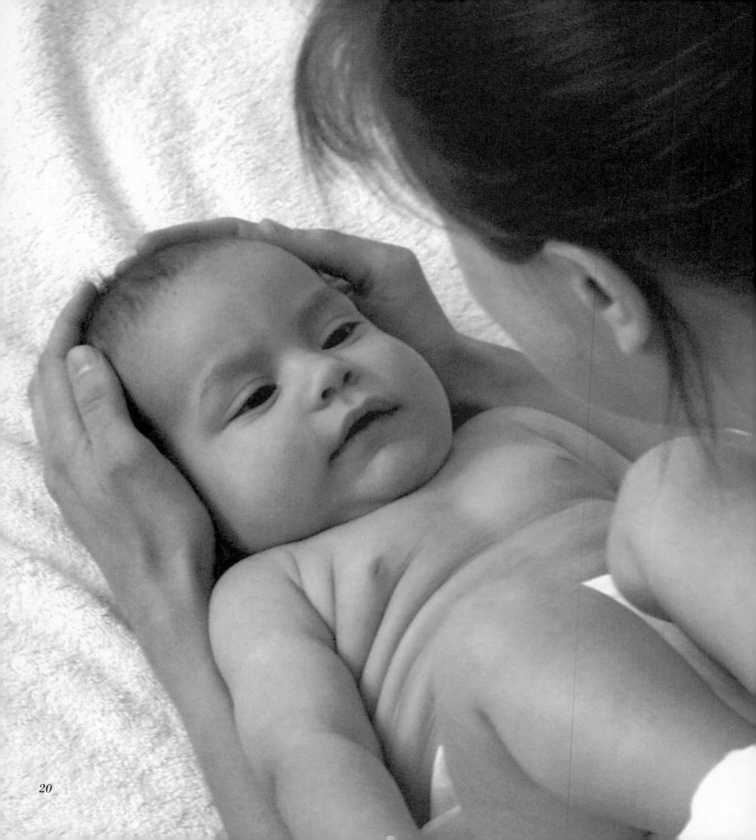

To be touched, stroked and massaged,

is nourishment for the child.

Nourishment as important

as minerals, vitamins and proteins.

Nourishment, that is love.

If a child has to relinquish it

the child rather wants to die.

And sometimes it actually does.

Frédéric Leboyer

The fetus

Let us for a minute remember, or imagine, life as a fetus. We are in a pleasantly tempered, soft and embracing environment. The sounds from our mother's heartbeat and breath are mixing with her voice and other sounds penetrating from the outside. Light is filtrating through the abdominal wall of the mother. We experience touch from the surrounding tissue inside the womb. The sense of touch develops early, and from the age of six weeks we react to sensations of touch. The bigger we grow the more we feel the pressure around us. We can even feel our mother stroking her belly from the outside. We learn how we can move so she can stroke our back while she is stroking her own tummy.

The birth

We are experiencing enormous and most obvious sensations of touch as the contractions start and we are pressured out through the birth canal. After an often long and overwhelming massage experience, we see the dawn of life and are expected to quickly adapt to a world very much unlike the one we have been dwelling in for the last nine months.

Thanks to empathic and clear-sighted people, deliveries today are done in as lenient ways as possible for both mother and child. I am happy that many children today are born in light-dimmed, heated rooms. Soft music, which the baby might have heard during the pregnancy, is played. Hopefully no chemical substances have been given to the mother and no electrodes have been attached to the baby. The taking of blood samples and other procedures that cause the baby pain, can be spared or kept to a minimum.

Delivery care has, in many countries, made huge progress in only a few decades. Therefore, let us hope that no newborn hereafter shall have to hang upside down, held by their legs, spanked and put onto a cold scale!

After a period of about two hundred and sixty six days in the womb, the human child needs the longest time of all mammals to develop. Birds quickly learn to fly, fish swim and reptiles crawl, but humans need at least nine more months before we can move our own bodies. The reason, why we come to the world in such an "immature" state, is that we have to be born when the head is proportional to the birth canal. If women were pregnant longer the babies would simply not get out! At birth our brains are only twenty three percent of the size of an adult's. The brain grows quickly the first six years, but even so does not reach its full size until the age of twenty. In comparison the brain of the monkey for example, is growing very fast in size and complexity. When a baby monkey is born its brain is already seventy percent of its final size. During the first six months the brain of the monkey grows the remaining thirty percent.

Thus, the newborn baby faces a long and important development period from the moment it lies helpless in our arms. Through the continuous stimulation of the skin, resulting from the vaginal contractions during labor, the life sustaining systems that need to function after birth are activated. This means that breathing, circulation, elimination (bowel movement), the endocrine system and the nervous system have been stimulated to start and function. The seemingly painful birth has been designed by nature to help the baby's body function once it is outside the womb. Babies that do not have a vaginal birth, but are delivered through caesarian section, will need compensation for the loss of the strong stimulation a natural birth normally gives.

"To Sam"

New, pink and wrinkled
You were born of my body.
Your fearless gaze searched me–and found.
During dizzying seconds when galaxies
And universe were created and died,
We met, touched and were united.
I slowly caressed your back.
In the touching of your skin
I could read the promises of the future. L.J.

Touch equals life

All babies have, due to their physiological immaturity at birth, a great need for touch. It is of vital importance that this need is fulfilled. Without touch an infant will die. We have known this fact for quite some time. Nevertheless babies around the world die because nobody holds them, hugs them or caresses them. There are orphanages where children die of isolation, in spite of sufficient nutrients. For survival, food is not enough. A small baby also craves contact and touch so its bodily functions and development can proceed.

Let me tell you the story about the German emperor Fredrik II. Back in the thirteenth century he wanted to find out the original and natural language of the human. Would a child who was not taught to talk naturally speak Hebrew, Greek, Latin, Arabic or the language of the biological parents? To find an answer to this question he took newborn babies and had them cared for by nannies. Strict instructions were given not to communicate with the babies in any way through words or babble. The nannies were supposed to only feed and clean the babies. No other contact whatsoever was allowed. The good old emperor never got an answer to his curiosity. All the babies died. They could not survive without closeness, touch, and joyful intercommunication.

Premature infants

Prematurely born infants are usually placed in an incubator. This technical and phenomenal invention has saved the lives of many premature infants. In spite of the fact that these stand-in wombs are as similar to the real thing as imaginable, it has been found that the tiny newborns do not always grow as quickly or develop as adequately with their use. In the process of designing this artificial womb some important details, which have a striking effect on the infant's physical state and rate of growth, have been forgotten. The incubator holds a temperature equivalent to the one in the uterus. Nutrients and oxygen are supplied for nourishment of the little body. So far so good. Nevertheless, if we would crawl back into the womb we would immediately notice what is missing in the incubator: the touch of the walls of the uterus against our skin, the rhythmic sound and pulsation of heart and lungs surrounding us, the familiar voice of the mother penetrating.

Almost accidentally it has been proven that prematurely born infants who are touched, massaged, talked and sung to – especially by the mother – show visible signs of more rapid growth and calmer behavior. Furthermore, if a tape with lung- and heart sounds is played, one will succeed even further in imitating the real state in the womb.

For pacifying purposes the previously mentioned tape can also be used for the full-term babies. It is not an easy change that the newborn has to manage, adjusting from the existence inside the mother to suddenly being separated and having her on the outside. Anything we can do to make this adjustment easier will help the infant to better adjust and develop.

In the last twenty years, a series of studies have been made on prematurely born infants and their reactions to massage. Over all, every study has been positive. A recent analysis has shown that 72% of all premature infants, who had received some kind of tactile stimulation, had reacted positively. Most researchers reported better weight gain and faster development in infants that had received massage. One study showed that the babies were more awake and active during the time of observation. This was confusing for the researchers since they expected the infants to sleep more in order to save their energy for growing. The massaged infants also showed better results on a special test scale (Brazelton). They could leave the incubator and go home almost a week earlier than the non-massaged infants.

One point of interest to note is that in studies where very light touch had been used the weight gain was less. It seems that too light of a touch is more irritating than stimulating to the infant. Most likely very light touch is interpreted by the nervous system as tickle, and therefore it does not have the same beneficial effect on the body that a firmer touch has. In those studies where they had found better results, a firmer, yet soft massage had been given. We believe in such cases that touch receptors as well as pressure receptors have been stimulated. If we reflect back again to what has been the natural habitat of the unborn we will better understand why the infant is more comfortable with firm, soft touch than with very light touch. Inside the womb the baby is firmly and softly held by the walls of the uterus. The fetus is experiencing both touch and pressure inside the uterus as well as later in the birth canal.

The Kangaroo Method has reduced the time needed for hospital care of premature infants. In the Kangaroo Method the infant is put skin to skin inside the clothes of a parent or a nurse. This method came about in Colombia to keep the prematurely born infants warm since there were not enough incubators to fill the need. The method is now spreading around the world. Developing countries have recognized that the Kangaroo Method is working well and that the body temperature of the infant can be kept at a satisfying level. Even if the infant is put in an incubator it is still worthwhile to occasionally carry the baby in a kangaroo manner as a means of feeding it with the body contact and the stimulation it needs.

Closeness and spoiled babies

As fashion trends change, so do trends in the raising of children. As a new parent I let myself be led and misled by various "experts" in the field. If there should be a rule in childcare the simplest, in my opinion, is to follow your own loving instincts. And if you want to use your head – study what is natural and genuine.

Today it is again accepted to hold and carry the baby all the time if one wishes to do so. Not too long ago the babies were disciplined early and not pampered with too much closeness. The babies were thought to get spoiled if their needs for touch, closeness, and nourishment were fulfilled. They were supposed to lie by themselves in a cradle or cot, preferably in separate rooms, and fed at certain hours. Dependent women have learned from books about childcare written by non-empathic men. This is true for many in the western world. In other parts of the world, where the motherly instinct and culture have remained, the babies have enjoyed, what in my opinion is the right thing, plenty of touch and body contact. No child, as far as I know, has ever been spoiled by getting its fundamental needs satisfied.

To swaddle and carry the baby – "The in-arm-phase" – The continuum concept

The habit of swaddling the infant during its first months was a practice we used to have in our culture, and still is a habit in some other cultures. Thanks to the study results about touch we have today we can see that this occurrence had its justi-fication. Although today the method is looked upon as a bit outdated. The procedure has been seen to deprive the baby of its capability of movement and the idea has been rejected.

The American writer Jane Liedloff has, during extensive travel in the jungle of South America, studied the rainforest Indians. She has observed how they live together and how they rear their children. It took her some time to put her finger on how the Indians were different from us, and furthermore to find out the mechanisms of these differences.

The biggest difference she found, in terms of babies, as they are our focus in this book, was that the Indian babies almost never cried. Colic pain in infants or sudden infant death (SID) was never heard of. The older children were never seen fighting, teasing, arguing or in any other way vindicating themselves. They seemed happy, calm, balanced and appeared to be functioning well in groups of children. Also they easily got along with the adults and were at a young age taking part in different working tasks together with the grown ups. (In parenthesis it can be mentioned that these Indians did not have a common word for work. Everything they do is done with a great expression of joy, with laughter and jokes, always in the company of others. Work for them is not associated with any kind of conflict or tension. It is done out of inner joy and willingness. There is no "must", constraint or aversion in the context of work.)

So, where is this balance, this joy of life and harmony cre-ated? How arises such a behavior and way of life that is free of conflict and naturally relaxed? Let us look back at the newborn baby. We assume that the newborn is expecting to have its needs fulfilled as they have been during the past nine months in the uterus. That includes changes of movements and posi-tions, light and sound stimulation, a surrounding temperature of about +37 degrees Celcius (98.6 degrees Fahrenheit), even flow of nutrients and last but not least, constant touching. If this is what the newborn infant expects, how may it then experience what it is usually subjected to after birth, and what consequences do these procedures have on the infant?

From a vertical position, with its head mostly down, rocked by the movements of the mother, the baby now mostly lies still in a plane, horizontal position. The ever-present sounds of the mother's heartbeat and breathing, mixed with incoming sounds from the outer world, are gone. In the cot, cradle or baby carriage –where the baby is lain not to be disturbed- there is no rhythmic beating, no familiar background sound, and no voice of the mother. The friendly pink light, the shadows and changes in the milieu (womb), have been exchanged for bars, a canopy or a hood, a surrounding that does not change color or form. The temperature has dropped at least fifteen degrees (C) and hunger, which the infant has never experienced before, is repeatedly attacking with excruciating pain. If the infant is lucky it is once in a while offered a warm and milk-filled breast as comfort which can still the unpleasant feeling in the stomach. If the baby is less lucky, the mother believes that the baby too recently had a meal and therefore it is most likely something else that is the matter. It has to wait for another hour or so. After a change of diapers it is again banished to its lonely place in the cradle or cot, and is covered with cool and stiff textiles, far away from warmth and touch, far away from everything that has been, and still should be, a natural existence for the baby. Yet we expect it to be happy and healthy, to sleep tight all night, to digest its food and without any fuss develop in a promising way.

For a mother in contact with her own intuition and her original instincts, this behavior and way of treating the small one would be as to rip off her own arm. To separate her and her little child would be as painful and physically tangible as actual mutilation. There is one place, and one place alone, that is right for an infant – and that is in the arms of its mother. If for any reason the mother is not available, the father, a sibling or another relative or engaged adult is the one to offer their arms. During its first six months, or until the baby is moving by itself, crawling and later walking, it should be held in arms, or tied to the body of another human being. In the group of rainforest Indians that Jane Liedloff was studying, the infants were from their birth, until they chose to investigate the world on their own, constantly in contact with the mother – skin to skin. This is what she calls the continuum concept.

When we consider the fact that the human being at birth is less developed than most other species, the continuum concept seems totally logical. To get the most natural continuation of existence, a womb-like milieu is the best suited. When the baby has reached the maturity it needs to voluntarily move its body, it is time to open the arms. At first, for a short while, let the baby investigate the surroundings by itself, and later extend the time according to the development and maturity of the baby.

Just for the fun of it, let us compare ourselves with the kangaroo. The little kangaroo baby is born the size of a pinky, worm-like and naked. Its obvious place is in the pocket on the belly of the kangaroo mother, where warmth, food and security are offered. Imagine how many kangaroos would survive if Mother Kangaroo got the idea, because she had read somewhere it was the trend right now, to leave her defenseless little baby in the grass. She would strut off to look for food or take a stroll by the big road to watch funny metal boxes on wheels.

We can see how risky such an abandonment would be to the defenseless baby. Nature has made sure though, that every species has built-in protective behaviors and instincts, and in some cases even special arrangements like the pocket of the kangaroo, to guarantee the survival of the offspring.

Conditioning

A way in which nature has assured keeping mother and baby together is through conditioning. As soon as the babies are born or hatched they are conditioned to the being in their presence. This makes them follow this particular being, most often the mother, which defends and feeds them. When the baby is big enough to take care of itself it separates from the mother and continues on its own way according to its line of development. The mothers are also conditioned to their babies. This conditioning is done at the moment of birth and the time following. It helps the mothers to separate their own babies from others.

The human race still has this kind of conditioning. Because the newborn human baby is born with such poor motor skills it has no way of following the mother. A remaining feature from our hairy days is the grip reflex. As our mothers nowadays are part of "the naked monkey tribe," there is no way for us to hold onto or even stay close to our protectors. To have any guarantee of survival it is of vital importance that the mother is strongly conditioned to the infant. Such a conditioning, and the need for it, is instinctively present in a normal and healthy woman who has a newborn. Therefore it is crucial and important that the conditions are right for this process. A woman that has the process of conditioning interrupted often experiences deep sorrow and a feeling of loss. This can result in depression, and also in delivery psychosis and breast feeding psychosis. It was only a couple of decades ago that we learned how important the first minutes and hours are for the parents and baby to bond and attach to each other. Parenthood is experienced more positively, and the baby is often calmer, if all parties have had the opportunity to peacefully connect. The reason why the baby is calmer and less demanding might be due to the amount of touch it is receiving. Parents who have bonded with their baby are touching it more, and are more likely to react better and more correctly to the signals of the baby. Through having the instinctive behavior more accessible, a "conditioned" parent better fulfills the needs of the baby.

Even if the mother had to deliver with a caesarian section, the baby could, and should, if possible, be placed on her chest to hear her heart beat and to smell her. If the mother is unconscious, one could still let the baby have this first, important moment fulfilled. Hopefully the father is also present. As long as the condition of the baby is not demanding otherwise, skin contact between the newborn and the parents should be the goal. If the mother has not been conscious during the labor Baby Massage is highly recommended in overcoming the loss of this first contact.

When early bonding has not occurred

Not always is the climax of a delivery a pleasant meeting between a wrinkled bundle and two overwhelmed parents. The wish would be to let the newborn, from its position on the belly or chest of the mother, peacefully enjoy the acquaintance with those people in whose arms it will be resting the nearest for the months and years to come. Maybe the mother is drugged and absent due to pain relievers. Maybe the father is so shocked by the bloody and painful labor that he is mentally absent. The father may also be hindered from physically participating. The midwife or doctor may find the newborn in need of an acute check up, something might be wrong, and the infant is hastily taken away for examinations and tests. Maybe it is put in an incubator.

When infant and parents for any reason have not had the opportunity to have the early bonding, Baby Massage has shown to be an eminent way of "finding" each other. Touch is the key word. For parents, who have grieved the loss of early contact with their baby, a solution to their problem can be found in massage, touch awareness, and co-sleeping (letting the baby sleep with the parents).

\

Adopted babies

Adopted babies and their parents have a special kind of situation. How can parents bond with a child they have not been conditioned to from the birth? How is the wound of separation healed; separation that the adopted baby has suffered from due to the disappearance of the biological mother? Connection is made, as we see, both ways; parents bonding to the baby and the baby attaching to the parents. Touching is the method, which can help unite and create the ties necessary for a solid and secure relationship.

A friend of mine has a beautiful adopted daughter, now a teenager. When this girl was adopted into the family she was about six months old. Her biological mother had been a drug addict and the baby had at birth traces of nine different drugs in her tiny little body. The doctors assumed she would suffer resulting defects such as mental retardation, if she were to survive at all. She survived alright, even after being in two different foster families before she eventually was placed in the family of my friend. In the care of my friend and her family the girl has grown and developed. She is now achieving higher than average results at school, and is also training in gymnastics with great vigor and balance. My friend is a very motherly woman with access to her intuition and instincts. She has shown great wisdom when it comes to children and their development.

When the girl had been in the family for about five years, my friend was not quite satisfied with the girl's attachment to the family. In spite of her developing nicely in every way there was still a weakness in her attachment to the family. She could, without much thought, go off with practically anyone who would ask her to join them. In a country where large numbers of children are daily lost without a trace, this was, of course, a problem. To try to do something about this behavior that eventually could prove to be a risk, my friend and her husband went through an "attachment-bonding program." During a two week period, the grown ups in the family took turns holding, carrying and sleeping with the adopted daughter. This assured that constant bodily contact existed between the child and the parents twenty-four hours a day. A belated continuum concept was created and performed. It was, of course, in the long run somewhat tiring for the three involved. But as they believed in it and thought it was important, they did not give up. It resulted in a better and deeper relationship.

The continuum concept put to practice

To a modern parent it might sound unpractical, not to say inconvenient, to maintain body contact with the baby twenty four hours a day. If we ourselves do not have the experience of such a tactile kind, we might not have the positive memories to support the transference to our own children. Can we get in touch with our own early preverbal memories; often do they turn out to be painful? Therefore it is not unusual that parents decide to give their babies what they did not receive themselves as kids.

What usually happens when two bodies are in constant contact is that they eventually are experienced as one single body. The surplus energy of the baby is discharged through the mother and her activities. From its protected place on her arm, hip or back the baby gets all the stimuli it needs. All senses (sight, hearing, touch, balance, smell, and taste) are triggered and trained. Babies who live their first months "in arms" of their parents are given the best conditions to become relaxed and happy.

Ever since human beings began standing upright, and thereby making the hands and arms free of the element of movement, it has been possible for us to hold our babies even when we are moving. However we are usually occupying our hands with other tasks than carrying the baby and therefore other ways have been found to keep the baby close to us. In my culture (Scandinavian) a carrier made of birch bark was common earlier. In other cultures it has been, and still is to some extent, a habit to swaddle the baby in a shawl or a piece of cloth, which was attached to the body of the mother. Often this piece of cloth could be a part of her clothing. A modern variant is a baby carrier, which nowadays is available in many different models. Using the baby carrier one can, from a relatively early start, carry the baby on the front. One drawback to these artifacts is that they are designed for the baby to be in a vertical position with its head up. This position in newborn and small infants can only be held for a short amount of time, and then with good support to back and neck. Otherwise the immature physics of the baby will be strained and exhausted. On the market, baby carriers are popping up that offer alternative carrying positions. Carrying cloths can be seen nowadays in our culture as well. They are practical in offering many different ways of placing the baby.

After initially having had the baby in the front of the body, close to food, heart sound and supervision, the baby can, after it has gained better tone and vigor, be placed on the back. For this purpose there are also special carrying chairs that can compensate for the baby carrier once the baby has outgrown it. Most baby carriers allow carrying the baby on both front and back. The bigger the baby grows the more it wants to participate in the world. The common steps of carrying positions are the following: 1) The baby prone on the chest/front of the person carrying. 2) The baby, supine on the chest, is facing out with its back to the front of the person carrying. 3) The baby sitting in a baby carrier or carrying chair, on the back of the person carrying. Both are facing the same direction. 4) The baby and the person carrying are back to back.

Anyone having held or carried a baby for a longer period of time knows how tiring it can become. The idea of carrying one's baby most of the time during the day might not be too tempting. One can wonder how an African mother has the strength to work all day in burning sunshine; carrying water and hoeing the fields, with a baby tied to her body. Is she built or made in a different way to better endure strain? That could be the explanation, but it is not likely that is the only reason. There are also other factors involved, which seem to make the difference between our sometimes rather weak performance, and their remarkable endurance. First of all, a baby, who from early on has had plenty of body contact, is more relaxed and adaptable. The baby becomes incorporated as a part of the mother's body. She does not need to parry or counteract the tension and resistance of the baby. Since the baby is placed closely to the mother's body, the bio-dynamics work to her advantage. To carry a baby of five kilos (11 pounds) close to the body is not as heavy as carrying the same weight in the hands. Secondly, people in tactile cultures are conditioned from early childhood to carrying their siblings. The body is better trained for the extra weight. And thirdly, people born and raised with a lot of touch have a lower level of stress and tension in the body. Thereby they have better access to their own muscle strength. Thus, they can better economize their resources.

Western mothers who have tried to live according to the continuum concept have stated that during the first days they

31

felt strained and restricted, but the longer they had their babies close, the easier and more natural it became. They also claim the relationship to the baby grew much closer. With the next baby they will not do it differently.

Co-sleeping

It is quite common to find that few babies sleep by themselves all night. When you ask around, it seems to be a rule more than an exception that both babies and children are waking up their parents at least once during the night. I remember my sister and myself, three and six years old, "performing shuttle service" between our bedroom and the bedroom of our parents. Our parents carried us back to our beds just to be awakened half an hour later by a child with an unfulfilled need of body contact. Eventually my exhausted parents gave up, and we were permitted to stay and enjoy the touch and warmth we subconsciously knew we needed. Even if a parent temporarily was sleeping elsewhere, his or her calming and comforting smell was still in the bed linen.

If the newborn baby is allowed to sleep with the parents from the beginning it will soon adjust its sleeping pattern to that of the mother. Consequently, they become well synchronized and their sleeping rhythm will coincide. This will assist the parent of an infant or a baby in avoiding being awakened repeatedly in the middle of a dream phase.

My son constantly awoke every other hour during the first three months. As I was awakened five to six times every night I never got the chance to finish my dreaming. Not only was I physically worn out by this nocturnal activity, I also thought I was going crazy. Waking a person several times during the phase of dreaming is a well-practiced torture method. My son, of course, had no such intention, and had I only correctly interpreted his communication and let him feel my presence more physically, we would have both had a better night's sleep.

A further benefit to co-sleeping is if the newborn infant is sleeping beside the mother it does not need to wake the whole neighborhood with its cries to have its hunger quenched. Instead, the infant can, with some assistance, sniff its way to the food and "grab a bite." Everything is easily available and in a ready to serve package! Since the mother to a baby with a synchronized sleeping pattern does not need to be shaken awake, she can rapidly interpret the baby's signals and offer it a nightly meal, usually without having to become wide awake herself. As they will both simultaneously go through the shallow sleep phase, the baby is more likely to feel its hunger during the superficial sleep period and will want to have milk. The mother then can easily offer it the breast. In this way both mother and infant will have a better sleep and a homogenous day pattern.

Most new parents, and new mothers in particular, experience the depth of their sleep to be shallower. They are alert and listening to every sound the baby makes. They jump out of bed, over and over again, only to discover a false alarm. Sometimes they have the urge to get up just to check if the baby is actually breathing. The longer the period of vigil and disturbed sleep, the less alert one becomes in actually getting out of bed to breastfeed, change diapers or put in the pacifier. Is it not much more comfortable to have the baby right next to oneself?

"I would never dare to have the baby with me in the bed. Imagine if I rolled onto it", says the dear parent. There is a risk, of course. From hearsay my great, great grandmother accidentally smothered one of her twelve children to death. But considering the pressure of frequent pregnancies and deliveries, a small house full of kids plus the responsibilities of farming duties, one can understand that exhaustion prevailed, and an infant was suffocated in its sleep by its mother's heavy, overtired body. So yes, it can happen! Normally we do have a natural sense of where the baby is even if we are asleep. This function may be non-existent, however, if the mother is under the influence of sedative medicine, drugs, alcohol or if she is totally exhausted. In my opinion, though, colic and SID are much more common than infants accidentally smothered. The positive effects of co-sleeping are clearly predominant in comparison to the risks, which according to my judgement (if precaution is taken) are minimal.

Babies that have spent the night in the beds of their parents from the start usually sleep still and peacefully. Fighting arms and kicking legs, on the other hand, is common in children having missed the "in-arm-phase." There is more tension in the touch hungering body than in the body of those that have from early stages experienced skin contact.

If you have a baby that does not sleep well during the night, you could let it sleep with you. You can choose to do so even with a child that has already passed infancy, however, you need to be prepared for a period of time for becoming accustomed to the new arrangement. Once the habit has been "broken in," both parents and children will enjoy the result of a sounder night's sleep. Babies, who during the night have the chance to compensate for the lost closeness to the parents, are more relaxed and happier during the day.

Older children that have been given the possibility of gaining back lost tactile contact with their parents, might after some time of co-sleeping move back to their own bedroom. In the presence of security the wish for independence comes naturally. There is a balance in everything. If we truly listen to our children they do signal and verbalize their needs clearly, and thereafter the only thing we need to do is to fulfill their desires to the best of our ability.

Infant Massage

Massage offers us constructive feedback on the need of touch in babies in general, and on their special needs in particular. If the baby is prematurely born, is born from a c-section, or shows defects or handicaps of some kind, massage is an excellent support to the physiological maturity and development of the infant. When it comes to ceasarian sections, the baby born from a planned ceasarian section is likely to need more massage, than the baby born from an acute c-section because the latter usually gets some stimulation through contractions prior to the actual operation.

Massage is beneficial, however, for every infant. It stimulates circulation and the immune system and promotes heart activity, breathing, and digestion. This recognition has over the last few years resulted in Infant Massage becoming more popular in the western world. Many new parents have heard about the method and some have even learned to massage their own babies. In numerous cultures in Africa, India, and the South Pacific, massage is part of the everyday care of infants and babies. In New Zealand the Maori mothers massage their babies to straighten out their legs and to improve the shape of their noses. To cure stomachache, the mothers in Cuba rub the tummies of their babies with a mixture of oil and garlic. On the Samoan Islands massage with coconut milk, flowers and grass roots, is said to cure anything from a baby's diarrhea to a grownups headache.

In New Guinea there is a saying: "The baby cries to be closer to the skin of the mother." There are needs which can be met by Infant Massage, therefore, the massage of the baby is so valuable. Apart from the physical effects Infant Massage creates, the massage also deepens the relationship between parent and child. The experience of being born leaves one with a great and sudden feeling of emptiness. After months in the womb the child is no longer protected. Through Infant Massage the baby's feeling of still having the mother as a protective shield can be strengthened, and the feeling of separation can be reduced. Every infant should receive massage on a regular basis to assist adaptation to life outside the womb.

To touch, hold and protect one's child is a natural thing to most parents. When the child is born the parents usually start touching it with their fingertips, to get acquainted. Later the touching evolves to holding and stroking with the full hand. It is known that the way parents hold their infants will influence it for life. A firm but loving way of holding and touching the baby mediates confidence and trust, whereas a tense holding fashion, with stiff arms and hard or frightened hands, may transmit insecurity and anxiety. Parents who develop their sense of touch through Infant Massage, and their sensitivity to the infant from the beginning, create a relaxed relationship with the baby and will find it easier to comfort it. The personality of the baby and its relationship to others will directly convey the security the baby develops due to this natural body contact.

The tie between mother and child is often talked about. I would also like to remind one of the importance of the interaction of the fathers with the newborn. A great deal of closeness to the baby is a natural thing for the mother since she is the one breast-feeding, but for the father there is nothing similar. Therefore a daily massage is a superb opportunity in developing contact and bonding between baby and father.

Good friends of mine had a beautiful baby daughter, Felicia. She was given a daily massage following a bath. The father did this after he came home from work in the evening. The baby thrived and the father got to know his daughter in a very special way. This little procedure of theirs built a healthy bond for the baby to grow from. She early on mastered her body movements and her verbal skills also developed extremely well. I will never forget meeting her at the age of one. I had not seen her for sometime and she had started walking since then. What struck me as most amazing was the way she walked. She had a balance I have never before seen in such a young child, and she moved her body with grace and stability. Today Felicia is a lovely four-year-old. She is a strong-minded and independent little girl with a loving relationship to her father. Not only her father gets to enjoy her brilliant company but anyone around can be amused by her social skills and wit. Anyone can see

the benefits derived from the rich tactile stimulation on her development.

Baby Massage - When - Where - How

When to start massaging

If you want to begin with baby massage you can step-by-step do so as soon as you have become acquainted with each other. Do not force the start but begin when the time feels right. In India, for example, it is common to start when the baby is about one month old. The most important thing is that you are close to each other as much as possible in the beginning. Remember it is not the massage technique that is most important but that you are touching your baby with warm, loving hands and with a total presence.

You can start massaging your baby even if it is a little older. It is not too late to start even if you get the idea of massaging your baby at a later stage or if you get an adopted baby that is not a newborn.

The best time to do massage

It is very individual when it will suit you and your baby in finding the actual time for massage. For some it might be in the morning after finishing the morning procedures, while others prefer a quiet moment in the afternoon or before bedtime at night. The best time may change according to the child's growth and varying sleeping and eating habits. It is important the baby is neither newly fed, nor hungry or too tired. Try to find a time during the day best suitable for the both of you.

When to interrupt or not to do the massage

Do not try to massage the baby against its will. It might happen the baby is not at all in the mood and dislikes the activity. The massage moment is meant to be a positive and relaxing experience for both of you. If the baby is clearly objecting through displays of persistent crying or other signs of discomfort, then wait. It does happen that the baby expresses itself through crying when tension is released. Remember that the birth is often a struggle for the little one. It may have been pinched or pressed during delivery and the memories activated through massage may be expressed by crying. If this happens the best thing you can do is to show your empathy and allow the baby the space and the time it needs to heal the painful memories. Crying is the only way of expressing pain and sorrow that the baby has, so just hold it and listen to the story told in its cries. Try massaging the baby again later or another day.

If a newborn has difficulties in maintaining its body heat, or if the temperature inside is not sufficient (less than 72 degrees Fahrenheit) it is not advisable to undress the baby for massage. Instead, keep it close to your body stroking it over its clothes on the body parts you can reach.

Where to do baby massage

The most important thing when considering the place for massage, is that it is a warm and draft-free spot. It may be done indoors or outdoors, on a bed or sofa, on the floor or ground, in your lap or on a nursing table. Whatever location you choose for massage make sure that you have soft bedding for the baby to lie on, preferably made of washable and natural fabric such as cotton. A thick cotton blanket covered with terry towels works well. If you choose to enjoy the warmth and fresh smells of being outside on a summer day, remember not to expose the baby to direct sunlight.

How often baby massage can be done

In principle you may massage your baby everyday. If you are aware of the baby's preference you will know when to shorten the session or when to rest for a day. If sometimes the breaks between massages may be long do not burden your conscience with that, remembering it must be pleasurable to massage the baby.

Older siblings may also ask for attention making it hard to find a quiet, peaceful moment alone with the new baby. In such cases it can be an advantage to have the father step in and take over the massage. Inviting the siblings into the massage may also be a success.

If you feel you are not having the time to massage your baby as often as you would like, remember body contact and closeness are the most important. You can still carry the baby and co-sleep with it.

How to best position yourself for giving massage

You have a great variety of alternatives to choose from when it comes to positioning yourself for massage. In the beginning during the baby's first weeks and months you may prefer to sit leaning against a wall or a backrest with your legs bent. If you are leaning against a wall you might want to put a cushion behind your back. In this position the baby can lie in the cradle created by your legs and lower abdomen. If you find it comfortable you can also sit with straight legs out in front of you placing the baby on your thighs.

If you choose to put the baby in front of you then you may also, for example, sit with straight, spread legs. You may also sit on your heels with your legs spread or together. If you are flexible and you find it comfortable you can sit in the squatting position, sitting between your heels instead of on them. In any case try to sit in a comfortable position using cushions to avoid too much pressure on your ankles and tail bone. Your position should be comfortable and restful enough to allow you to maintain it throughout the whole massage without being bothered. Do also think of bending forward from your hips instead of crouching over to prevent tiring your back.

If you are giving your baby massage at a nursing table try to stand as close as possible. You will have better eye contact with the baby and your working position will be better as well.

How to prepare for baby massage

Once the right conditions for time and location are found, you will then need to get some extra towels. The baby might urinate or even have a bowel movement during the massage, but this is a sign of relaxation and should not be reacted to negatively. An extra diaper to put on afterwards should always be available. For the baby that has started to discover the world and therefore has a hard time lying still, an interesting toy might come in handy.

Last but not least, the massage oil should be easy to reach. Maybe you have made time to heat it in the microwave oven or in hot water. (Caution! Make sure the oil is not too hot. Always try it on yourself first.) You may, of course, massage without oil but research has shown that babies react better to massage with oil. When it comes to oil it is of great importance what kind of oil you use for massaging your baby. The skin of the baby is delicate and products that could harm their tender integument should not be used. Virgin vegetable oil is the best choice and there are many different vegetable oils to choose from. Light oils such as safflower, thistle, and grape seed oil are suitable to use for baby massage. Shea butter, avocado, olive, sesame, and jojoba oil are, in the order mentioned, fat to semi-fat alternatives. Apricot oil, peanut oil, almond oil, and macadamia nut oil can also be used, but should be used with care if hypersensitivity or allergies to nuts runs in the family. Wheat germ oil is fatty and rich with vitamin E and can, since it has a strong smell, be mixed with other oils. During hot summer days coconut oil and safflower oil can be used since they have a cooling effect on the body. In wintertime the babies can be massaged with mustard seed oil mix or sesame oil, which have a warming effect.

One reason why it is important to use clean, vegetable oil is because the baby may suck on its hands. Whatever we use to massage the baby could then enter its digestive system. Vegetable oils are easily digested by the human body since the structure of the fat in the oils is very similar to the structure of the fat in the human body. Many oils and lotions marketed for babies are, unfortunately, made of mineral oil. That oil is derived out of a non-organic petroleum compound. Mineral oil is difficult to absorb and has a tendency to cover the skin like a film and clog the pores. Therefore, for the sake of your baby, avoid all such products that contain mineral oil (such as Vaseline and paraffin based products).

Before you start massaging you want to warm your hands, take a deep breath, relax and ask the baby for permission to massage it. Establish eye contact and ask the baby out loud, "Would you like a massage?" It may seem illogical but it acts as a signal that the massage will be on the terms of the baby.

Beginning the massage in this manner will allow for the baby to respond with its wishes.

How long to proceed with baby massage

For infants under the age of one month the massage should not be longer than ten minutes, otherwise 15-20 minutes is usually an optimum amount of time. Once you are used to the routine you can stretch it to half an hour, if you and your baby feel like it. Stop before either of you finds it boring. It is important that the massage is associated with a positive experience.

If the baby enjoys massage you can continue throughout the infancy. In India it is common for infants to be massaged daily until the age of six months; thereafter they are massaged less frequently. The baby, in fact, never gets too old to be given a massage. As the child ages it will move from baby massage to child massage, and later in life Swedish massage or other bodyworks will be used to assure continued health and well-being.

How to give massage when the baby starts walking

The massage might need to be adjusted when the baby moves to motor development stages and does not find it interesting to lie still long enough to be massaged. You might need to massage the baby in a sitting position and in a more playful way. Sometimes only short sequences will do and in some phases of development the baby simply will show that it does not have time to receive a massage. There are so many other things to discover and learn about. Do not insist on massaging the little one if other things have higher priority. Instead try using the spontaneous moments of closeness and cuddling, which occur during the day. It is perfectly adequate to stroke the baby on top of its clothes while it sits in your lap or is put to sleep. Sometimes one needs to take a break from massage. Usually new phases occur in the baby's life when both physical and psychological support and tactile stimuli are needed. It is then you need to be there with your hands full of love and presence.

How to massage babies with special needs

Babies with special needs may benefit greatly from being massaged. For babies with mental tardiness, physical handicap, hearing impairment, blindness etc. massage can have a positive impact.

You can massage a baby with a handicap the same way you do with a baby without a handicap. If stroking under the foot triggers reflexes and tension in the legs you should instead stroke more on the edges and top of the foot. For babies drooling a lot and breathing through their mouth, facial massage, especially around the mouth, is good. If the baby is treated by a physical therapist you may ask him or her for more advice regarding your child.

Blind babies have shown to develop better when the tactile sense is trained through full body massage. Pay attention to keeping skin contact with the baby throughout the massage and talk to it explaining what you are doing. Even a deaf or hearing impaired baby should be talked to in a soft and loving way during the massage session. Eye contact is of great importance and should be kept as much as possible.

Adopted infants may also benefit significantly from the contact created through baby massage. For both parties massage may be one way of learning to know each other.

In some children hypersensitivity or tactile defense may be seen. These hypersensitive babies, who react with dislike when touched, should be massaged with firmer pressure. Through starting with short sessions, concentrating on pressing and stroking the body with a terry cloth, the brain can be helped to better organize. Often one can overcome hypersensitivity through perseverance and slow transitions from pressing and holding to gliding strokes with the palm of the hand.

Premature babies can be massaged as soon as they have reached the weight of 1000 grams (2 pounds 2 ounces). Take it easy in the beginning and start by only holding the baby's body parts. Relax yourself and share peaceful relaxation with your baby through your hands. Talk to it and encourage it to let go of tension and relax. Reward the infant when you notice a change. After holding and practicing the relaxation technique for a couple of days you may start massaging lightly with oil.

Infant colic and intestinal gas are painful for the baby. The situation may also be frustrating to the parents who powerlessly have to watch their baby in obvious pain. Massage can ease light gas problems to full blown colic. It stimulates the gastro-intestinal tract to function better. Along with massage, carrying the baby and checking the diet of the breastfeeding mother are suggested. Gas forming foods should be avoided; milk and gluten should be eliminated from the diet to see if that can help cure the ailing baby. (See appendix 1 for further help.)

How to start

Start by getting to know one body part at a time and then adding a new one each time you massage. This will give the infant a chance to get used to the massage. In the beginning you may be totally unpretentious, aiming for just spreading the oil on the tiny body. When you get into the habit of using your hands and fingers you might want to try some of the strokes described on pages 44-55. Eventually you can increase the massage to cover the whole body. You may also start by massaging legs and feet when changing the diapers. The abdomen should not be massaged until the umbilicus has healed.

Baby Massage
from A to Z

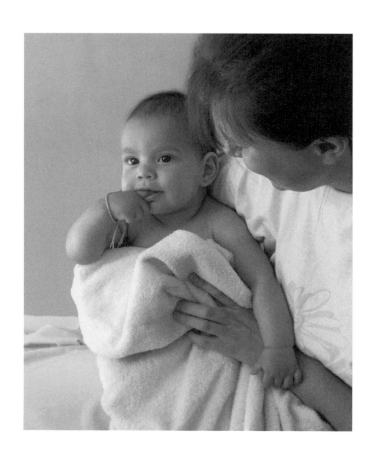

Introduction

In the following pages (44-55) you will find a suggested massage routine for infants. You may repeat each stroke from a couple of times to as many as the baby seems to enjoy. Remember that the enjoyment of touching, communicating, and being together with your baby is what counts. After having asked the baby for permission, you start by taking its clothes off and lying it on its back. While holding your hands around its head you establish eye contact. Relax.

Massage with an open, warm heart, talk and sing to your baby and get lost in each other's eyes.

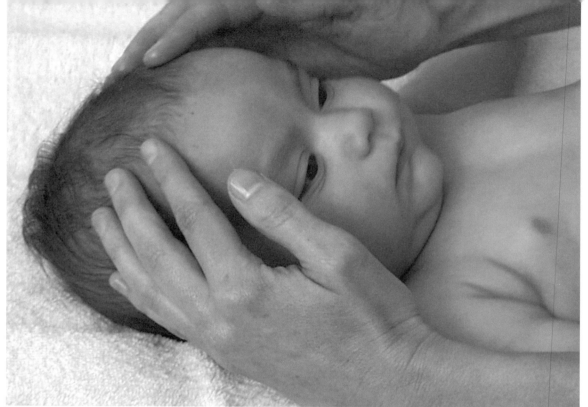

A. In a slow and relaxed manner start circling with your fingertips lightly on each side of the fonta-nel *(be extremely cautious here!)* and down the sides of the head.

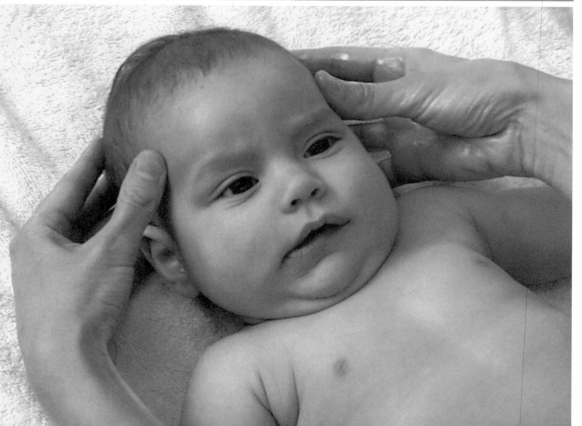

B. Stroke the forehead from the middle outward with your thumbs or fingertips.

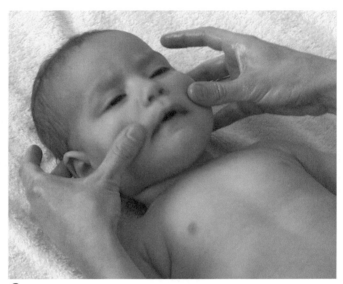

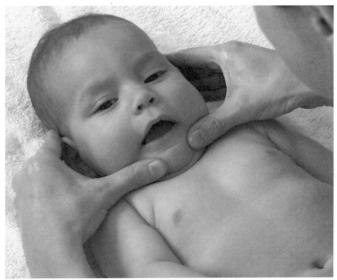

C. With your thumbs stroke from the root of the nose down the sides of the nose to the corner of the mouth and across to the ears.

D. Stroke from the tip of the chin along the jaw.

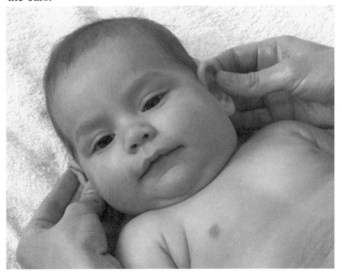

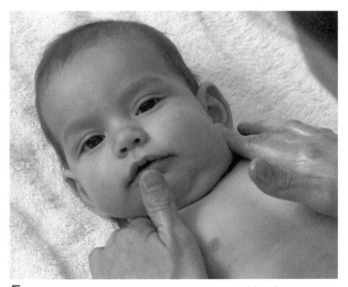

E. Rub the ears between thumb and index finger.

F. Put the ears between the index and the third finger and glide down the sides of the neck to the shoulders.

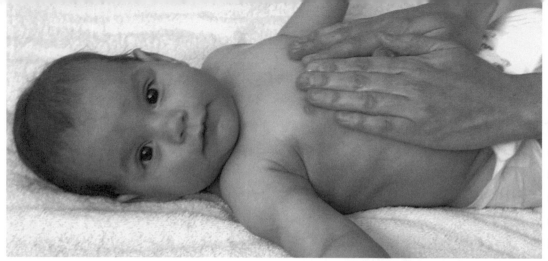

G. Stroke from the collarbone down the chest and abdomen to the pubic bone. Glide to the sides and stroke up to the armpits. Let the hands meet again on the chest and repeat.

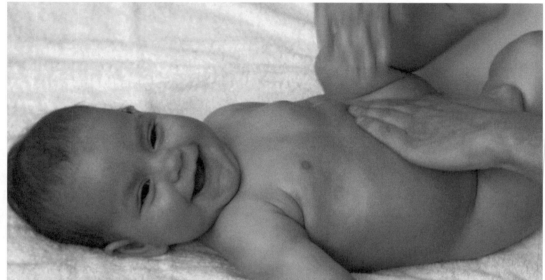

H. Circle clockwise around the navel.

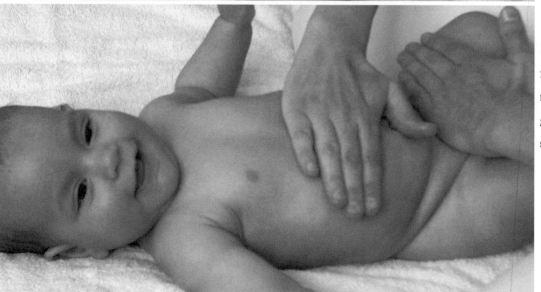

I. Do alternate strokes from the arch of the ribs down. Include the genitals without empha-sizing them.

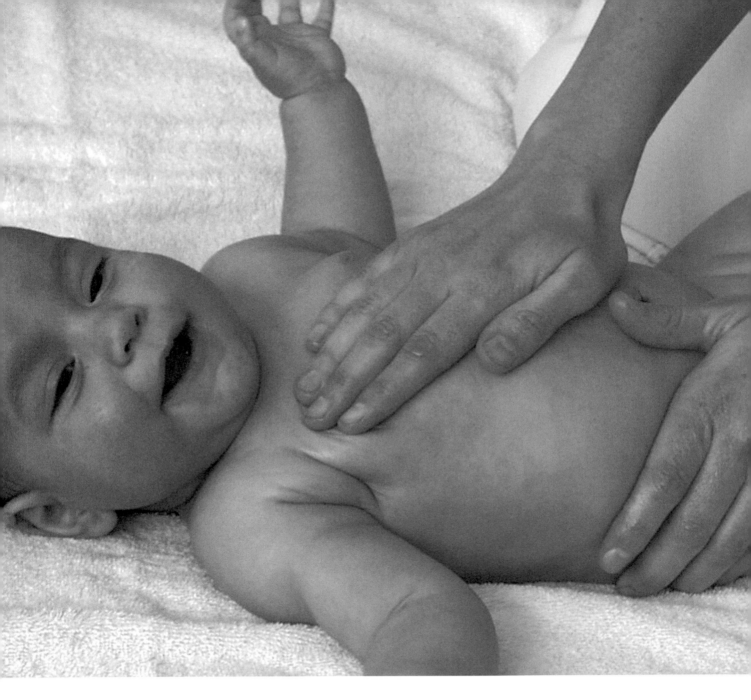

J. Stroke diagonally from hip to opposite shoulder. Alternate.

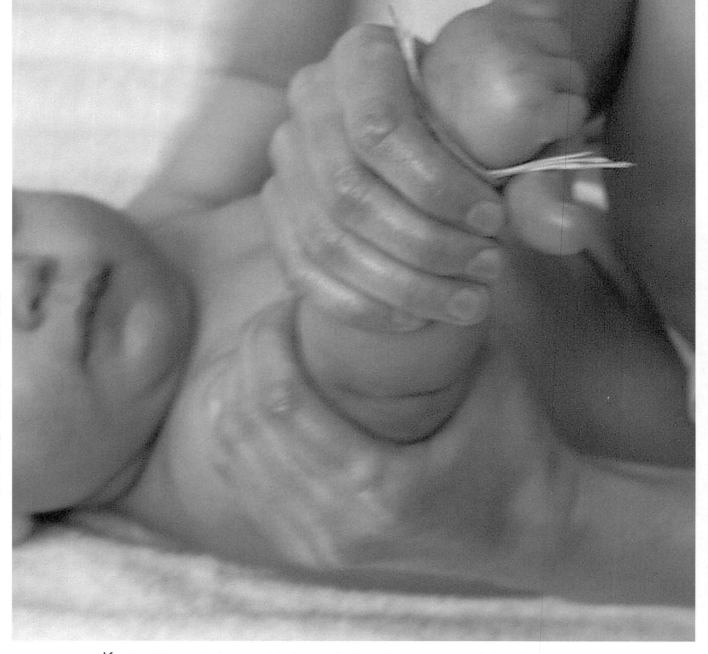

K. Carefully stretch the arm of the baby and glide with your other hand, formed as a pipe, from the shoulder to the hand. Repeat with your other hand.

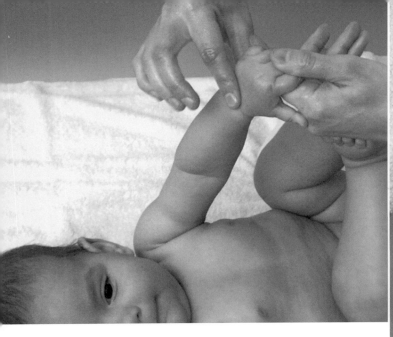

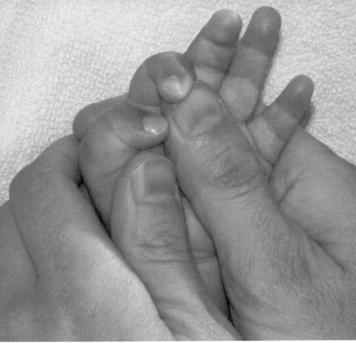

L. Make small circles around the wrist.

M. Stroke the baby's palm with your thumbs to open it.

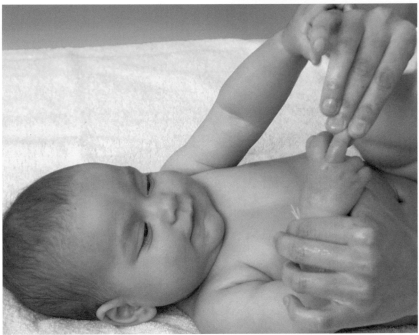

N. Lightly massage each finger. Tell a finger rhyme.

Repeat from **K** to **N** with the other arm and hand. End with stroking both arms simultaneously from shoulder to hands.

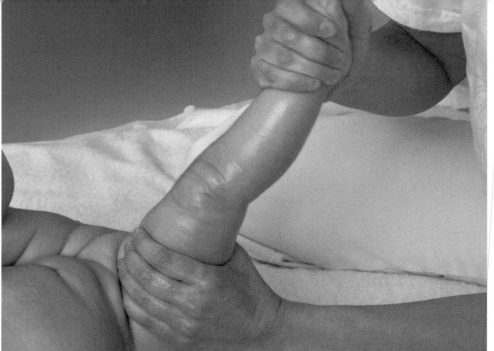

O. Glide with your hand formed as a pipe. Start at the groin and stop at the foot. Repeat with the other hand.

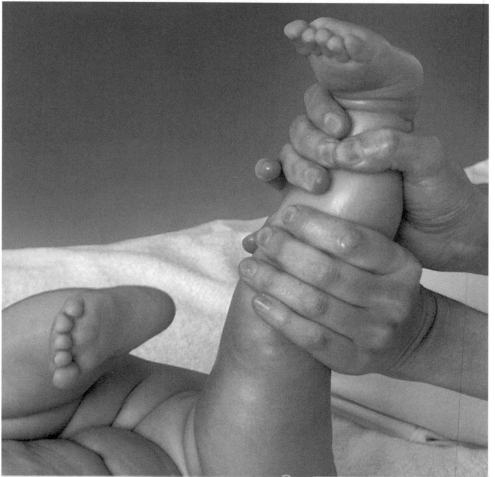

P. Hold the thigh with both hands. Glide in a screwing motion towards the foot.

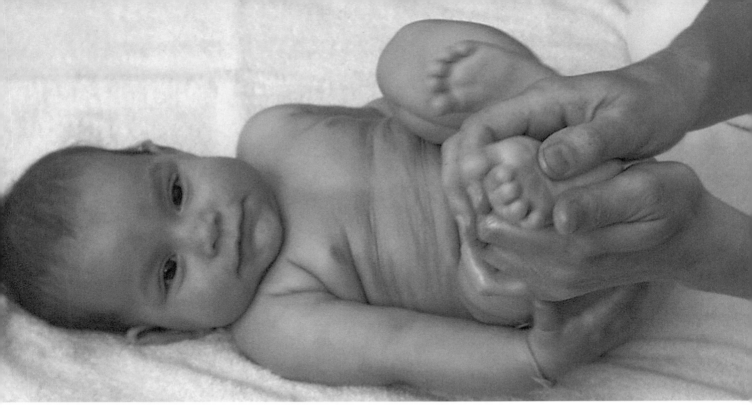

Q. 1. Stroke with your thumbs under the sole of the foot.

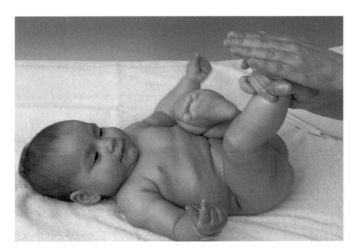

Q. 2. Hold around the ankle with one hand stoking the sole of the foot with the palm of your other hand.

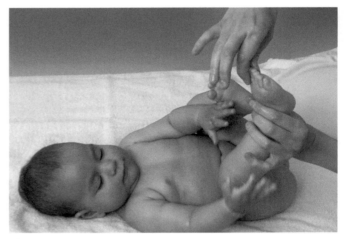

R. Roll each little toe lightly between your index finger and thumb.

Finish the front with long strokes from top of head to toes.

Turn the baby over on its abdomen and put him/her in front of you on a blanket or across your thighs.

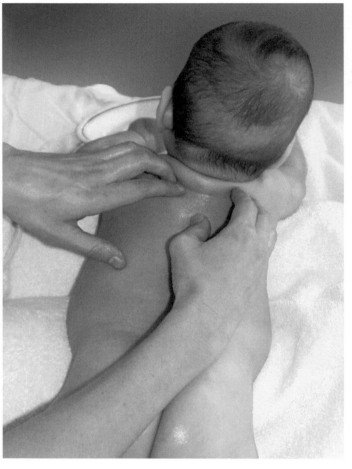

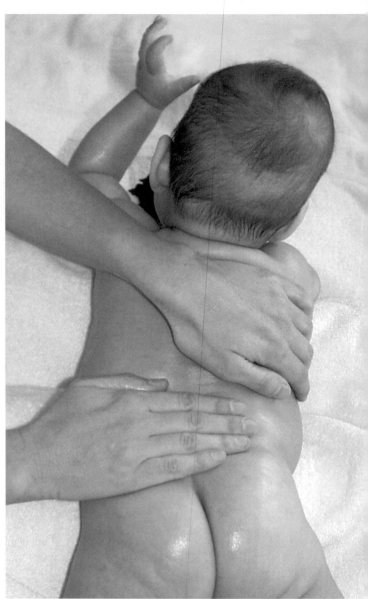

S. Start by circling lightly with your fingertips on the back of the head, neck and shoulders.

T. Stroke with your palms from side to side across the back.

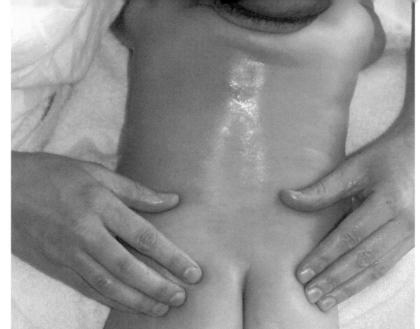

U. Circle with your fingertips on the sacrum and buttocks.

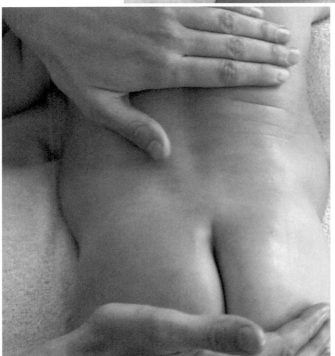

V. Stroke the back from neck to buttocks. Support with the other hand on the buttocks.

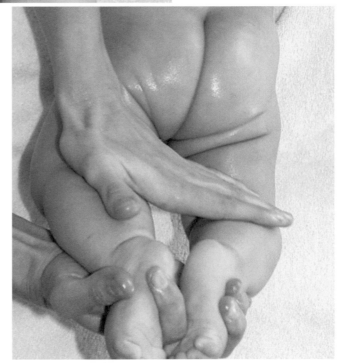

Finish the back by stretching the legs and holding them with one hand while stroking from neck to feet with the your other hand.

According to the East Indian tradition of infant massage, a series of light stretches are done at the end of the massage to further relax the muscles.

Stretching

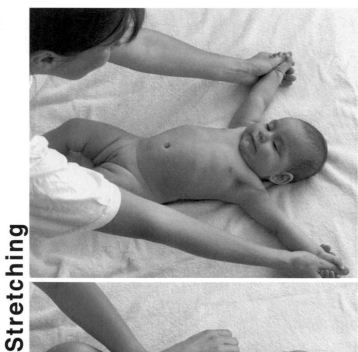

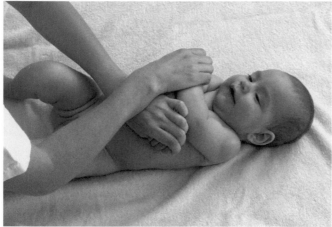

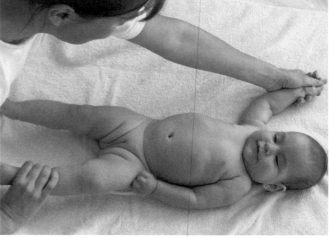

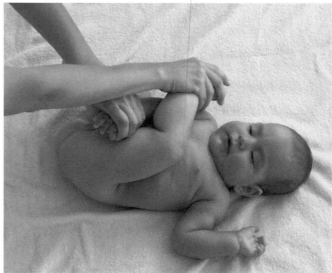

W. Grasp the hands of the baby and stretch them out to the sides. Then cross the arms on the chest. Repeat.

X. Grasp the baby's one hand and opposite leg. Make a diagonal stretch, then cross the arm and the leg across the chest so that the foot goes to the opposite shoulder and the hand touches the opposite buttock. Stretch out again and repeat with the other hand and foot.

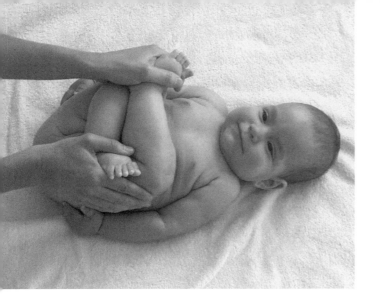

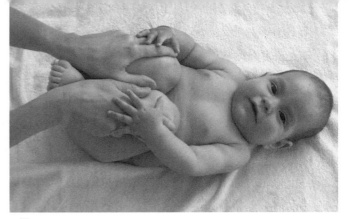

Z. Press the knees of the baby towards the abdomen and stretch them out again. Shake the legs lightly if the baby does not want to straighten them. Repeat.

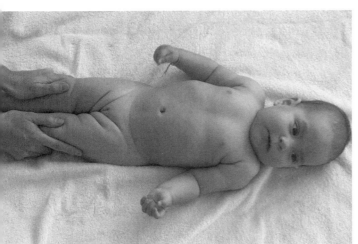

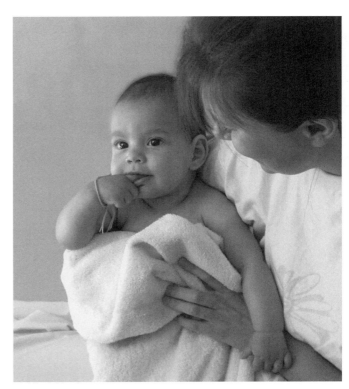

Y. Cross the legs of the baby in a cross-legged position and push them gently towards the abdomen. Keep them there for a moment. Stretch the legs and repeat by crossing the legs the other way.

End the whole massage by holding the baby, draped in a blanket, in your arms. Just be close for a while, enjoying your baby with a grateful heart.

Children's need
for touch

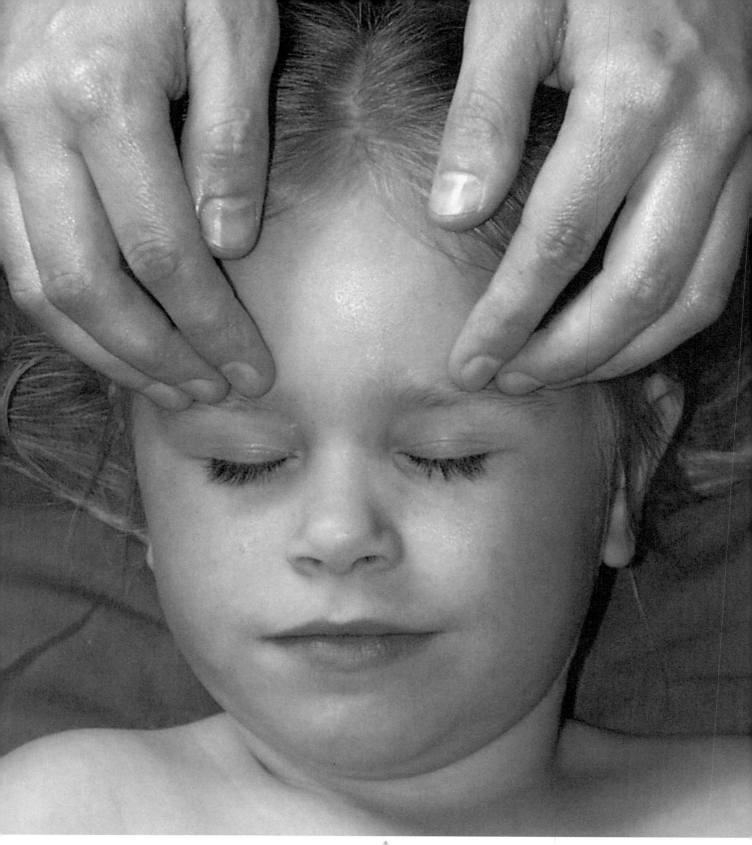

You, beloved child of the world

Come rest in my embrace.

Be strengthened for your journey,

To find the next resting place.

- L.J.

As clearly shown in the previous chapter, I speak warmly of abundant, early touch and close contact. Unfortunately however, reality indicates that the fulfillment of touch in most children is never truly satisfied. They therefore grow up with a hunger and longing for human closeness and warmth.

A toddler, who does not acquire sufficient amounts of touch, may show symptoms of increased fussiness, displayed through clinging onto the parents and demanding to be held and carried, and through poor sleeping patterns. There are many phases of development and maturity a child has to pass through. These, physical and mental phases can also be characterized by similar dissatisfaction and fussiness. Interestingly enough, in observing people from natural tribes, where lack of touch is rare, such behavior is seldom found. They seem to pass through most ordinary phases of development with less pain and confusion than the rest of us.

Kindergarten – the first big trial

A big step in the life of a small person is beginning kindergarten or day care. After being at home with a parent for the first years, the youngster is suddenly alone and separated from the closeness of the family. This step requires a great deal of courage and trust from the child to get through the process without friction. The initial introduction to kindergarten or day care normally takes a couple of weeks. Sometimes everything goes smoothly right from the beginning. The child runs off playing and does not pay attention to the presence of the parent. If the baby has a stable and secure foundation, coupled with an out-going personality, it may turn out to be the parent that has the harder time separating! But all too often the first weeks of schooling can be painful for both parties.

Separation is one of our most common and painful trials in life. We are separated from the mother at birth as soon as the umbilical cord is cut. Depending on how long and how often we find ourselves in the state of loneliness and separation, and how we perceive it, determines the varying strengths of which we express our feelings of abandonment and agony. To leave the child in day care can bring back memories of early abandonment in the parent, and anguish might become the symptom.

Child massage for children in day care and pre-school

Daycare and pre-school personnel have, in their role as substitutes, a tremendous contributing influence to whether or not the parent decides to go back to work after some time of being at home. This group of individuals, together with the parents, set the foundation for the child's life. The formative years are the grounds for future development. In many industrialized countries, children spend the majority of these years outside of the home. However, a happy and fulfilled baby will most likely grow in a positive direction, whereas a child, that lacks support and is forced to deal with too much hardship and pain, is more likely a candidate for the criminal register or the health care department.

It is important that those persons periodically substituting for parents are not too many; in other words, the personnel should not be exchanged too often. Young children cannot manage repeatedly attaching themselves to new individuals. This is especially true in cases of early separation. It is also of relevance that the substitutes are experienced and knowledgeable regarding the theories behind children's reactions. To establish close contact with the child, and to compensate for the separation from the parents, childcare personnel should not hesitate to touch and hold the child.

Programs supporting continuing education in massage for personnel in day care, kindergarten, and pre-school are gradually spreading in Europe. Teaching methods focus upon how conscious touch can be of help in the everyday work with children. In groups, where massage has been added at naptime, or in directed tactile games, there has been a noted change among the children. A tendency to increase their ability to concentrate has been seen. Children, who at gatherings or during story telling have not been able to sit still, can after a short period of touching on a regular basis, remain in their seats.

Touch stimulates communication and when a child feels it is heard and seen it does not need to be loud to get attention. The staff often experiences that the general atmosphere becomes calmer and that the sound level in the day care center decreases. The caregivers also feel that the massage calms them as well.

Children, who have seemed shy and silent, can all of a sudden entrust themselves to a chosen member of the staff. It is important, though, to remember, never to force touch upon a child. Some children might not want to be touched, and that has to be respected. Usually the child will show when it is ready to participate in the group's massage activity or in the tactile games.

In day care centers where children have a foreign language as mother tongue, touch and massage has been valuable. It is frustrating enough to be little and away from Mummy, but additionally not understanding the language spoken by playmates and adults serves to make the situation even more difficult. Through massage and touch, contact and trust can develop and a common language can grow.

Massage is most valuable for children to compensate for separation and lost parental quality time. Even though the teachers in pre-school and kindergarten do a great job with the children, it is, after all, the parents who are the most important grown ups in a child's life. Trust and expect that the teachers will provide the best learning environment possible for your pre-school child, but take full responsibility in being there for your offspring. Your undivided attention and loving strokes when you are with the child will make it possible for it to benefit the most from the learning experiences when left at pre-school.

Children receiving massage from adults will soon want to give massage in return. It is not unusual that the grown ups will start receiving massage by little, soft hands. Some children massage each other on their own initiative. They play and imitate different adults and their different touches as they massage each other. The children are creating their own tactile games.

Tactile games

Games where the players touch each other have been popular throughout the centuries in most cultures. Instinctively children have recognized their needs and thereafter invented games where touching is involved. Even rhymes and songs have been attached to the games. Touching and learning do go hand in hand. Thus, it is easier to learn a song or a rhyme if simultaneously the skin is stimulated. Body songs are typical examples of this. In these songs, words are learned as different body parts are touched. At the same time the children acquire a better awareness of their own bodies. In other words

it increases their body awareness. The children learn where different body parts are located, how they feel and how they are placed in relation to each other.

Other situations where the sense of touch is stimulated are, for example: facial painting, finger painting, modeling with clay, and kneading dough. All these activities stimulate the tactile sense and develop the child. To be rolled in a blanket, then pulled or carried, is a game the children play for fun while subconsciously stimulating self-awareness and contentment. In the same way, lying in a hammock stimulates the sense of touch.

Children with excess energy, disturbed body awareness, late speech or a low activated immune system, can be encouraged by tactile games. This can include anything from body contact games to playing with tactile tools or toys. Sometimes the right thing for a child can be the seemingly rough play with the father or a male adult. To be playfully elevated, twirled, and wrestled stimulates the tactile sense, giving sense of location and therefore balance. This is of importance for sensory integration.

Tactile tools

All touching carried out through a medium, an external object with which one touches, also can be called touching with tactile tools. Most of us have at some time drawn a grass, a cotton wad, a small paintbrush or a feather across the face of a friend or a family member. As children we love to feel and collect experiences from different kinds of touch. Many things we learn, and are given a word for, we first register with our sense of touch.

When consciously working with touch a whole list of tools for tactile stimulation can be found. We just mentioned grass, feather, paint brush, and cotton wad. All these can be used to increase our consciousness of light touch. If one were to make a list of tactile tools on a scale from rough to light, the previously mentioned objects would rate relatively high up on the list. The lightest touch, however, is the stimulation of air in moderate motion. Moving air–light breeze and wind–must be the lightest experience of touch imaginable. To experience the effects of a pleasant wind one need only go out on a warm but windy summer day or, if living in a climate zone with cold winds, blow on the skin with a hair dryer. I heard that in one kindergarten, children were blown dry with a hair dryer after having a bath or playing with water. The kids loved it, and in one sense received a double touch experience, since water is another medium through which light touch can be expressed. Luke warm water sprinkling and running down the body is an intense stimulation of the tactile senses. Water games, where the children shower, spray, and pour water on themselves and each other, are appreciated by most kids.

It is soft and pleasurable to stroke a furry skin or a stuffed animal. Soft fabrics and skins also give light stimulation of touch.

The next step on the scale of touch intensity is touching with hands, the most excellent tactile tool available. We communicate through the way we touch. To be touched by hands is a tactile experience, and to touch another is one, too. Hands can vary the pressure with which they are touching, and so they are the most flexible tool of all. Stroking with the hands on the skin or through stroking on top of clothes creates different sensations of touch. Apart from offering a certain quality to touch which other tactile tools cannot always give, hands can also send messages of which the giver is not always aware. We have the ability to express so much with our hands. We can comfort and encourage, show empathy or push away. Everything we feel for each other can be expressed through touch. With this in mind it is of great importance, that people working with children truly feel like touching them and massaging them. If there is resistance in the person giving, the receiver will feel it in some way or other.

Balls of different materials, wooden massage tools shaped as animals, hand puppets, roller pins and even toy cars may be used to touch the children and stimulate the tactile senses. These items may be woven into games, where they are rolled over or stroked on the body of the child or around its contours. This sensitivity training can also be combined with other kinds of body awareness exercises where the names and functions of the body parts are taught.

To gain a different, rougher quality to the touch experience, brushes, loofa gloves or sandpaper may be used. Brushes can be made of different bristle stiffness. Both the hair and the body, with or without clothes, can be brushed. The sandpaper may be touched with fingertips and hands, the loofa glove can be used dry on arms and legs, or wet, lightly rubbed on the back.

The list can go on and on, just let the imagination lead you. The most important thing of course is that the children are having a good time, and that they do not hurt themselves or each other. Pain is not part of the event. Tactile tools should only be used for positive aims to broaden the child's spectra of experiences of pleasant touch.

Sensory integration

A very important part of a child's development is sensory integration. Touch is a part of the process. Even if this subject is a little outside our main focus of touch, it feels important to examine it at least briefly.

Sensory integration means neural organization of the senses of sight, hearing, touch, and balance. The ability of the brain to organize these impulses varies from child to child. It is au-tomatically done in most children and therefore the ability is taken for granted. However, not all children's brains manage to localize and sort the sensory impulses correctly. This dysfunction may lead to learning disabilities, even though they are of normal IQ. Behavioral disturbances may also occur in some kids, despite good parents and a healthy social environment. Therefore the ability of sensory integration can have a great impact on the individual.

The senses integrate in four floating levels and in a continuing process from infancy through the preschool years. It is important that the first level is integrated well since the following levels are built upon it. The first level integrates touch, balance, and proprioception. All these senses are stimulated when the baby is carried for example. Correct interpretation of touch is needed for the baby to feel safe and to enable it to build emotional relations. The sense of balance has to function to enable us to move the body in a safe way. Proprioception relates information about the position of the extremities and the level of tension in the muscles. If the brain has not managed the first level of sensory integration, the child will move with jerky movements, have low muscle tone, and insufficient balance, in spite of well functioning muscles and nerves. The child may compensate for this but will later in life most likely be slower and tire quicker than others.

The second level is achieved when impulses from the tactile sense, one's balance, muscles and joints, are interpreted and organized correctly in the brain. This implies emotional stability, good body image and coordination between the halves of the body, well-balanced movements and good concentration ability. When this is functioning well, then there is a basis for processing sight and hearing impulses in an adequate way.

On the third level, the prerequisites for learning to speak and understand a language should be formed. Sight impulses are integrated to the three other basic senses. Thus the ability of the child becomes more defined. It can move through the room, climb, build with blocks, do puzzles and so forth.

During the last phase of sensory integration, the fourth level, the eye and hand specialize. The child is then ready to start school. Being able to concentrate on the schoolwork demands good organization of sensory impulses in the brain. Lack of sensory integration may create obstacles for further learning and development. If there are disturbances in any of the phases of sensory integration before the child starts school, it may effect the child's scholarly performance. A brain that does not manage to organize sensory impulses will have difficulties organizing numbers and letters.

Children experiencing a sensory integration dysfunction may be misunderstood and their learning disabilities and behavioral disturbances may be misinterpreted. Parents and caregivers do not always manage to understand that the disturbed behavior and the difficulties the child has are due to neurological weaknesses that the child can do nothing about. The problem is in the brain of the child and with help and support from the environment these disturbances can be neutralized.

As a parent or caregiver one can identify shortages of the sensory integration by recognizing symptoms of hyperactivity or concentration deficits. These symptoms are obvious and disturbing since the child cannot sit still or concentrate on anything. It runs and jumps around and finds it hard to know what to play with. In school the behavior may continue with the child displaying a lack of control. It may seem careless and fidgety, forgetting to do homework or bringing books and writing tools to school.

Sometimes the child may seem more difficult and fickle than other kids. It may be fretful and feels uncomfortable with both family and playmates. Usually it cannot manage to play with other children and instead ends up in disputes and sabotages the play. The child is hypersensitive to normal demands, shows bad self-confidence and hates to lose. It does not freely share with others and is easily hurt. It may even act aggressively.

Delayed speech development can also be a symptom of a disturbance in the sensory integration. Additionally, the child might have a low muscle tone and become tired quickly. It sits like a sack, having a hard time keeping its head in an upright position and therefore supporting the head with its hands while sitting. If the child has to stand for a longer period of time it will lean against something. Balance and coordination are poorly developed, which makes the child stumble easily, drop things, and in general seem clumsy.

If children show fear of taking the stairs, falling, swinging, riding on the merry-go-round, turning a somersault or doing any other physical activities where changes of the position of the head are involved, it may suggest a flaw in the function of the sensory integration.

Learning at school may be problematic. The child may be distracted or over-stimulated by light and sound around it and therefore, cannot concentrate on a given activity or be attentive in the way it is expected to. The child does not know how or where it should draw a line with the pen. Coloring inside lines can be very difficult. If the brain is not mature for learning it is useless trying to teach a preschool child reading and writing. First the child needs to participate in activities that stimulate the brain the right way, making it ready for school subjects later.

To prevent and treat disturbances in the sensory integration

As we have now seen, shortages in sensory experiences can be an underlying cause behind quite a few problems hindering our way to normal human development. I purposely touched on the subject of sensory integration in order to point out the suffering and the problems that may occur as a result of insuf-

ficiently functioning sensory integration. One should keep in mind however, that some of the symptoms listed may also be due to other factors that occur during pregnancy or delivery, or during the first years of life.

Play and daily activities are normally sufficient stimulation for a child's brain in the early years. When we notice that is not the case and the child is showing symptoms of dysfunction it is important to allow the child a chance to heal. It is not the symptoms that are the problem, but the irregular and ineffective processing of sensory impulses in the brain. What the child should be offered is massage and tactile experiences, a setting to roll, jump, twirl, crawl, run, pull, swing, balance, and climb in. Sensory impulses are to the brain what food is to the body. The child will know best what it needs. The brain is constructed to seek experiences that will develop it. In our society, unfortunately, the intellect is rewarded. Young children are all too often glued to the screen of a television set or computer. Instead they should be outdoors swinging and climbing trees. The only thing the brain wants is rich stimulation of the senses, and therefore I, once again, want to stress the pros for the continuum concept. This concept offers most of the stimulation our brain is hungering for – tactile stimulation, pressure, balance, position, light, sound and smell impulses and information from muscles and joints. With a healthy start it is easier for the child to continue the sensory integration in a satisfactory way.

One of the cornerstones for the development of the brain is tactile stimulation. Therefore, massage and touch should be a natural part in a child's life. There should also be time set aside for the children to train balance and movement, preferably outdoors in a natural setting. With all due respect to special teachers and learning techniques–if the organization of the brain is weak it does not help to give the child "a knife and a fork" when "food" for the brain is what is missing.

Child Massage – When-Where-How?

When to start child massage

If you are a parent or a grandparent and you are interested in massage, you have many opportunities for supporting the development of your children. If the child has received baby massage, it is likely to be used to touch and probably already has a good body image and body control. A child that has little experience of tactile stimulation might need to get used to receiving a massage, but will eventually enjoy and benefit from it as much as the child with previous massage experience. There is no particular deadline for starting child massage; whenever you feel like it or there is a need, you can start.

When not to massage

There are occasions however, when one should not give a child massage. First, if the child is ill or is feverish, it should not receive a massage, and secondly, of course, when the child does not want one.

Massage is always on the terms of the child. If you are turned down, you have to accept it. It may happen that the child is reluctant towards massage when it is first introduced to it. Among others, I know of one boy who definitely did not want to participate when it came to massage. He observed the daily massage activities on his siblings for two weeks. Eventually one day he decided to take part. Then, he wanted to do it again and again. It is wise to let the child decide for itself when it is ready to participate in massage. Even if a "no" always is a "no", one should never stop asking. One day the "no" can mature to a "maybe" and eventually transform to a "yes." There is yearning for contact in every child.

Where to best perform child massage

The massage can be performed wherever the child can lie down to rest. A mattress on the floor, a bed, a sofa or a massage table will do. If the parent has back problems, the massage table is the best choice. A mattress on a table may do as well.

How to start

For parents initiating massaging a natural way to begin is to combine it with the evening procedures. It is a good way of relaxing after a hectic day and it prepares the child for a sound sleep. If you are in the habit of telling a story you can catch two birds with one stone through telling a massage story. Different strokes are done on the back of the child simultaneously as a story is told. (See page 72)

Another convenient occasion to include massage is after a bath. Oil can be applied and the child can be massaged as an extension to the bathing routine.

Grandparents can even massage their grandchildren when the right opportunity occurs. If family get-togethers are rare, being massaged by a grandparent can become a ritual each time the child and grandparent spend time together. And even if not given regularly, massage will strengthen the sweet ties between grandparents and grandchildren.

How to deal with children with special needs

Some children have special needs due to congenital or acquired physical and/or psychological weaknesses or damages. These may vary in severity. Most children with a handicap benefit from massage. For kids with tactile hypersensitivity or extreme hyperactivity, it may be more difficult initiating massage but it is nevertheless just as good for them.

Tactile defense, which occurs in children with, for example, brain damage or autism, may reveal itself through the child's not wanting to have body contact. The child does not want to participate in tactile games, it does not want to wash or cut nails and hair, it has self destructive behavior such as biting and scratching itself, and it does not like to wear clothes or it wears clothes in many layers. Children with tactile defense can experience touch as unpleasant or even painful. Naturally, hypersensitivity may even occur due to negative tactile experiences.

If the child cannot tolerate skin to skin contact one may try to find another form of touch that is acceptable. Often stronger pressure and stroking works for a shorter duration and sometimes a light touch may be the only technique which is accepted. In the beginning try holding and massaging on top of the clothes. It is recommended to try out different tactile tools as complements in the process. If you start touching the child regularly within its borders of tolerance, these may slowly widen. The positive effects of the sedation give feedback and whet the appetite. By regular tactile stimulation with an acceptable touching technique, the nervous system tends to correct the unbalance that has ruled and the hypersensitivity decreases. Children who have previously withdrawn from body contact, may after a longer period of time of regular tactile training, manage to receive and enjoy massage with oil on the skin. In an American study where autistic children received massage, the hypersensitivity in the children decreased and they became more attentive and related better to their teacher. Attention spans also increased.

Children with high muscle tone and spastic muscles usually benefit greatly from massage. The mother of an active and happy seven-year-old boy with cerebral palsy took part in one of my classes in child massage for parents and caregivers. She was asked to rate the muscular tension in her son before and after massage. The son made a rating of himself. The mother told me about the son's response: "He feels really great after the massage. When I ask him if he can get more relaxed he says no. He rates himself to be a ten (on a scale from one equaling very spastic to ten equaling normal muscle tone). Also, his elimination has never worked better than it has during these weeks of regular massage."

Children with DAMP (Deficit in Attention, Motor control and Perception) or ADHD (Attention Deficit Hyperactivity Disorder) may need to be physically active prior to being touched or massaged. Remember it should be on the terms of the child. It is important to observe the reactions of the child and to approach the situation with the greatest sensitivity. Find the places and the kind of touch the child accepts and start there. Let the child lead the way. Once confidence is established you may eventually be able to meet skin to skin.

When massaging children with special needs it is advisable to create a routine and do the massage accordingly. The same routine should be repeated every time so that the child can recognize and predict what is coming. In this way order and safety is created for the child, which is important for most children with brain damage.

Spina Bifida is something some children are born with. The symptoms are loss of sensitivity and muscular function in the lower extremities and usually also in the pelvis. These children are bound to a wheelchair but differ in no other way from normal kids. (It might be good to remember that all children, despite handicaps, are more alike than they are different from each other). In spite of the lessened or lost tactile sensitivity in the lower extremities in children with Spina Bifida, leg massage can be beneficial as well as enjoyable to them. Due to decreased circulation, the legs easily get swollen. Massage can help increase the circulation and prevent swelling. There is no reason to exclude paralyzed body parts on someone with functional or sensitivity loss. The body still is a whole and should be treated as a unity, including all parts.

Appreciative receivers of massage are children with Down's syndrome. One problem these children have is that they stick out their tongue and drool a lot. Massaging the face, especially around the mouth may to some extent reduce the problem. In children with Down's syndrome low muscle tone is also displayed frequently through hyper flexible joints. If the child has difficulties controlling its body movements due to low muscle tone, massage can be given with a focus to stimulate, tone and activate the muscles. This may be achieved through stroking towards the heart in a faster tempo than usual. Pumping pressures over the muscles and light Tapotements (hacking) can also be done.

In studies, massage has proven to help children with asthma, diabetes and rheumatoid arthritis. The asthmatic children experienced improved pulmonary functions had fewer asthma attacks, and were less anxious and sad, after having received massage. The kids with diabetes, who were massaged by their parents, also had lower anxiety and depression. In addition, their glucose levels decreased to the normal range after one month of massage. Positive effects were seen in children with juvenile rheumatoid arthritis, too. Besides less anxiety, they also experienced less pain, especially at night, and the morning stiffness lessened in the kids as well. In all studies parental anxiety and feelings of helplessness also decreased.

It is not necessary for a child to be diagnosed for it to need tactile stimulation. Every child that seems nervous or anxious, is clumsy or has delayed motor skills, has late speech and language development, is gloomy with little appetite, or is unhappy and crying a lot, needs warm, safe, aware adults who touch it.

How long to continue with child massage

As a parent, you can massage your child from the time it is a toddler through childhood and into adolescence, until it leaves the nest. The massage techniques can be changed to suit the growing body of the child. The chest stroke should be excluded for girls after the age of eight, or earlier if they say so, since some enter adolescence early. It is important to support the integrity of the child and let it own his or her body. It is always with great respect and honor we touch and massage small children as well as older ones.

Each session may be anything from 5 minutes to at the most 45 minutes. The upper limit is stated to avoid over stimulation of the nervous system. As the child gets older, you may stretch the limits a little. It is preferable though, to do short frequent massages instead of long infrequent ones.

How to prepare for child massage

Once you have decided to perform child massage the room should be prepared. Dim the lights, make sure the room is draft free and warm, light some candles and put on some peaceful music. It is good if the music is slow and harmonious. If you are massaging a child with brain damage, it is better to start without music. Later, when the child knows the routine, music can be added. In any case, the music should not be too loud. Make sure your hands are clean and warm. Take off any rings, jewelry or watches that could scratch the skin of the child. It is also best to have short fingernails. Roll up long sleeves that could be in your way.

In the beginning, the massage can be executed on top of the clothes. As soon as it feels comfortable, you may offer the child a massage with oil on the skin. To choose the oil, please look under chapter "How to Prepare for Baby Massages" page 37. If you want, you can use essential oil to stimulate the smelling sense. A few drops are dropped into an aroma lamp, or mixed directly in with the oil. Mandarin or lavender essential oils seems to suit most children. If the child has brain damage, it is best to avoid essential oils since the child might be hypersensitive to smells and odor.

For younger kids a special massage blanket and pillow can make the massage moment even more special.

As giver of child massage you should be calm and focused and have a great will to touch with a glowing, parental heart.

Massage stories

Massage stories can be told to any child who loves a fairy tale. The massage is given simultaneously and enhances the story. On the next page is an example of a massage story that has been appreciated by both young and older children. It can be done with the child either sitting up or laying down.

Once upon a time there was a summer land.The sun was shining bright and warming all the flowers, trees, animals, and people.

Do big strokes on the back.

One day clouds were flying across the sky and covered the sun and the whole sky. It all became overcast.

Do soft palm press all over the back.

Then it started blowing, first just a little bit and then more and more. A real fall storm was blowing. The trees were swaying and the leaves were twirling in the wind.

Stroke with fingertips freely like the wind on the back.

It began raining. Big raindrops fell from the sky and made the whole land wet. Everywhere on the ground were puddles and the children jumped in them.

Drum with fingertips on the back.

As it grew colder the rain turned to snow. Beautiful snowflakes slowly came floating down from the sky. Soon everything was white. It became really white, really quiet and really peaceful.

Drum lighter and slower.

The only thing one could see was a little kitty cat climbing up a hill…
And one more…
And one more that climbed the highest hill.

Walk with two fingers up the side of back to shoulder.
Repeat the other side.
Walk up the spine to the top of the head.

There it sat down and started purring.

Circle with fingertips in the hair.

It sat on the hill until the sun returned and started warming the land all over again one more time.

Big strokes on the whole back.

72

**Child Massage
from A to Z**

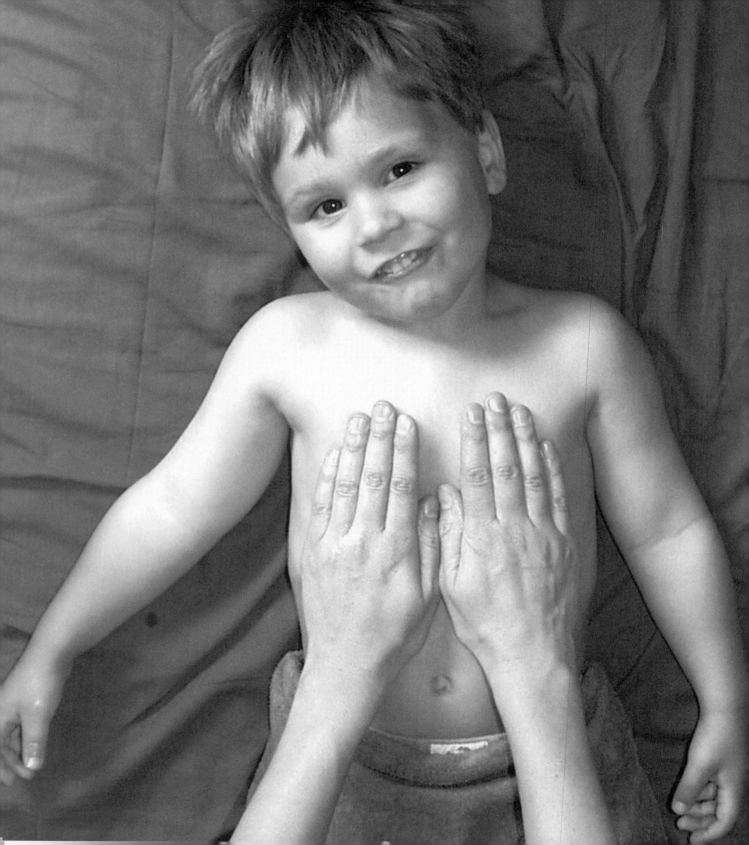

The following is a suggestion for a massage sequence for your child. You can use these massage strokes from the early years of childhood through adolescence. Remember to communicate with the child so you will learn what it prefers and likes. Also allow quietness for resting or for letting things be expressed. Keep an open attitude and healing will occur.

Begin by asking the child if it wants a massage. If the answer is positive, ask the child to lie down on its stomach in the place you have already prepared. Make sure the child lies comfortably and is covered with a blanket or a towel. Take a couple of deep breaths, relax and get ready to start massaging. Think of using the whole palm of your hand when you do the strokes. Every stroke should be repeated at least three times before changing to the next. You do not need to put pressure on the muscles when massaging. The weight of your hand is enough. It is also important not to let go of the touch between strokes. Keep contact the whole time during the massage!

Start and end each body part by holding it for a moment, counting to three. When one side of the body is finished, or the arms or the legs are massaged, a so-called connecting stroke is done. That means, for instance, that the whole backside is stroked in one long stroke. This will help the brain to draw a clear body map. After having massaged separate parts, we connect the body to a sense of wholeness.

Always keep the body covered, only exposing the body part you are massaging. It is important not to get cold.

Following are sequences for a full body massage. You can, of course, do the massage partially or take the body parts in a different order if you wish.

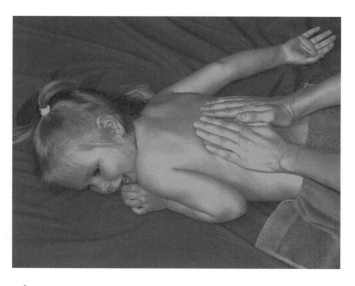

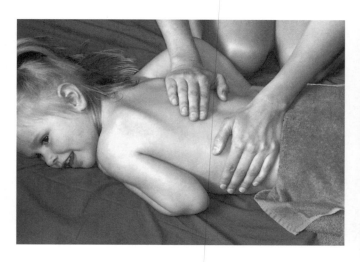

A. Place your hands calmly and gently on the back. Start stroking up the back with both hands parallel. Glide down to the lower back and repeat the "swim stroke."

B. Make strokes across the back, from side to side. Work with your hands alternating so that one hand strokes the right side of the back and the other hand the left side. Alternate.

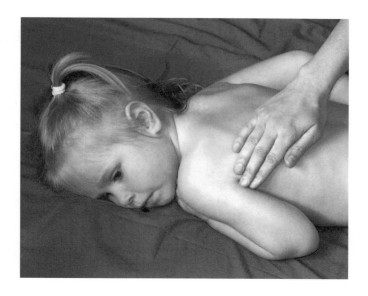

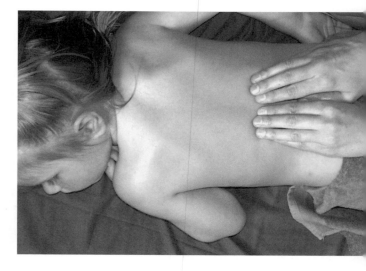

C. Do big circles around the shoulder blades, one at a time.

D. Circle with your fingertips in small "swim strokes". Start at the base of the back and work calmly upward to the neck and all the way to the base of the skull.

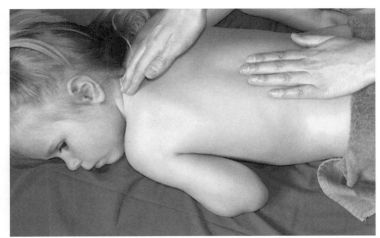

E.   Glide down the middle of the back from neck to lower back. Let one hand follow the other.

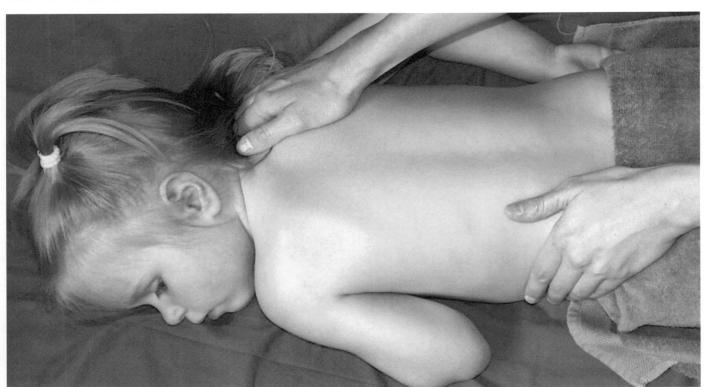

F.   Place both hands on the middle of the back. Stroke diagonally having one hand stroke to the shoulder and the other hand to the opposite hip. Let the hands meet at the middle again and repeat the other diagonal. Round up by holding your hands still on the back for a while.

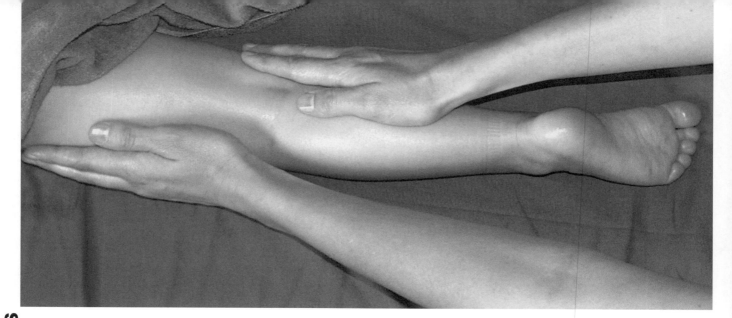

G. Stroke from the foot up the leg. Let the outer hand stroke all the way up to the hip. The inner hand steers across from the inside of the thigh to the back of the leg a bit before the groin (the upper third of the thigh is a private area and therefore omitted). Glide lightly back to the foot and repeat.

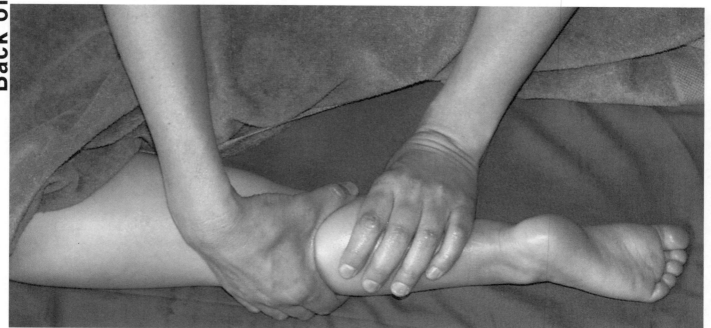

H. Shape your hand as a C. Make alternate strokes across the leg, up and down.

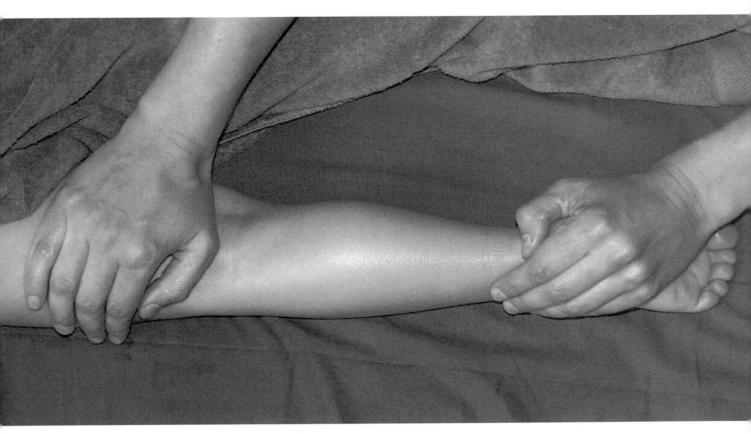

1. Stroke from the hip to the foot. Remember to keep contact with one hand at all times.

Repeat all strokes on the other leg. End the back of the body by doing connecting strokes from the top of the head down to the heels. You can stroke on top of the towel or blanket. Ask the child to turn over on its back.

Now have the child turn over and repeat from **G** to **I** on the front of the legs.

J.
Make circles around the kneecap and the knee joint. Glide to the foot.

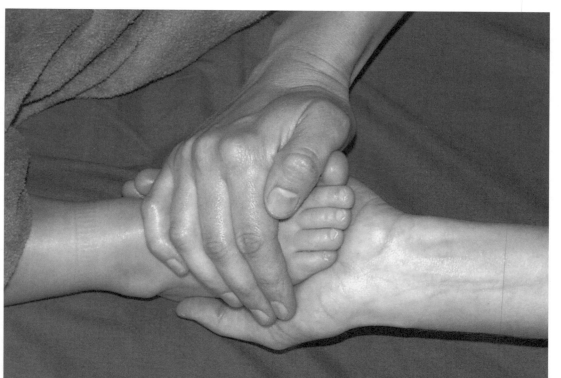

K. Hold the whole foot and stroke it up and down.

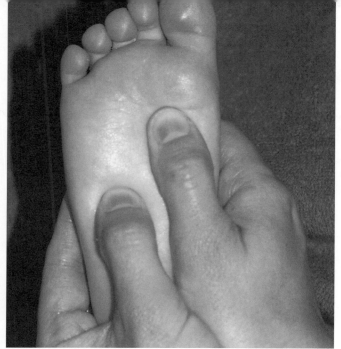

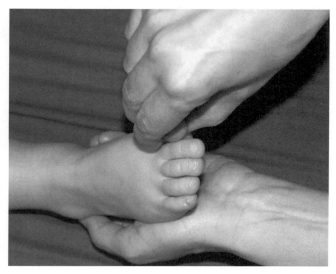

M. Gently rub and hold each toe.

L. Administer light thumb pressure under the sole of the foot.

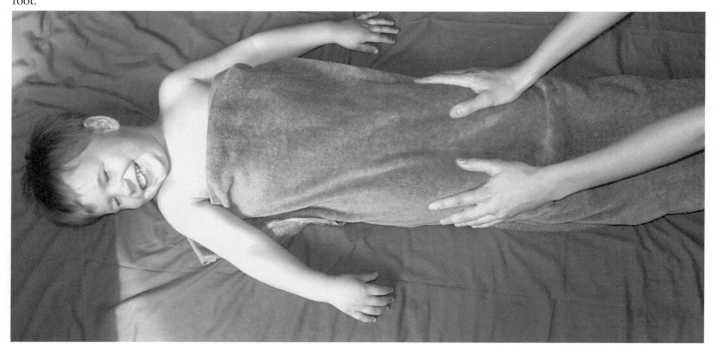

When both legs are massaged, make connecting strokes on top of the blanket from the hipbone to the toes on both legs simultaneously.

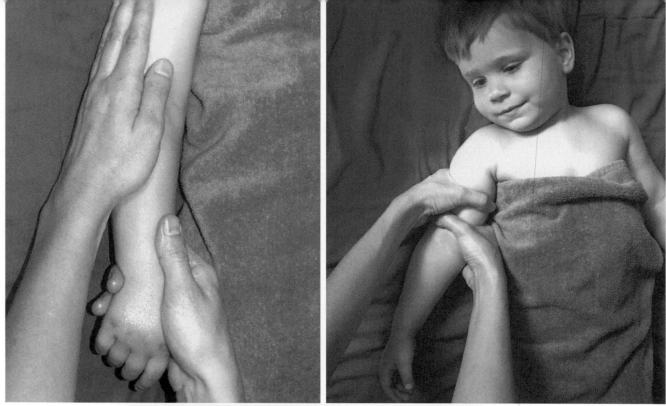

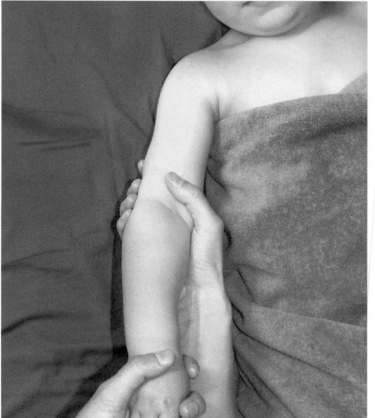

N. Hold the wrist with one hand and stroke with the other toward the shoulder. Change hands.

O. Shape your hands as a tube around the upper arm. Glide down the arm in screwing motions.

P. Stroke down the arm from shoulder to hand with one hand at a time.

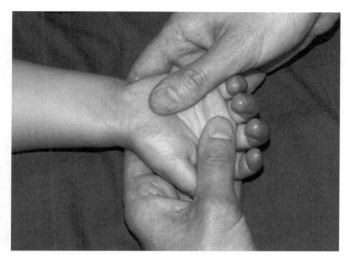

Q. Stroke the back and the palm of the hand.

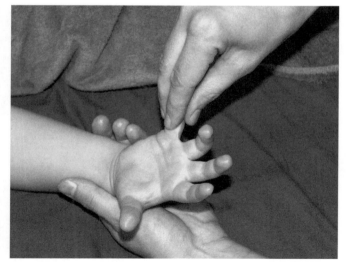

R. Carefully rub and hold each finger .

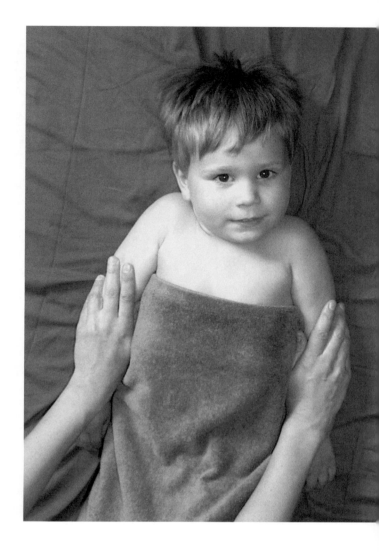

Repeat from **N** to **R** on the other arm and hand. Then stroke simultaneously both arms from shoulders down to the fingertips a couple of times.

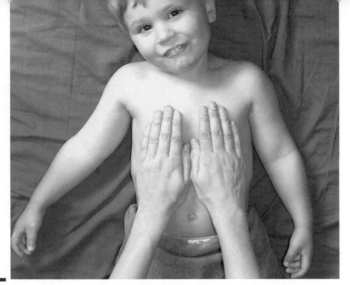

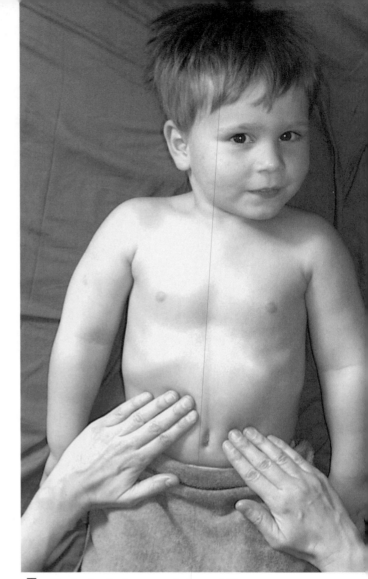

T. Circle clockwise around the umbilicus.

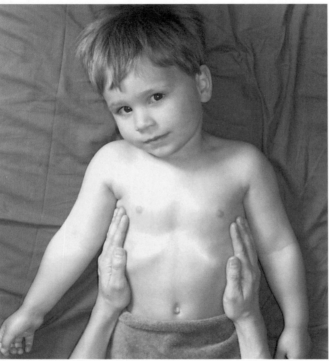

S. Do a backward "swim stroke" from the chest down the abdomen. Glide lightly up the sides to the armpits and repeat. (For older girls you can exclude this stroke).

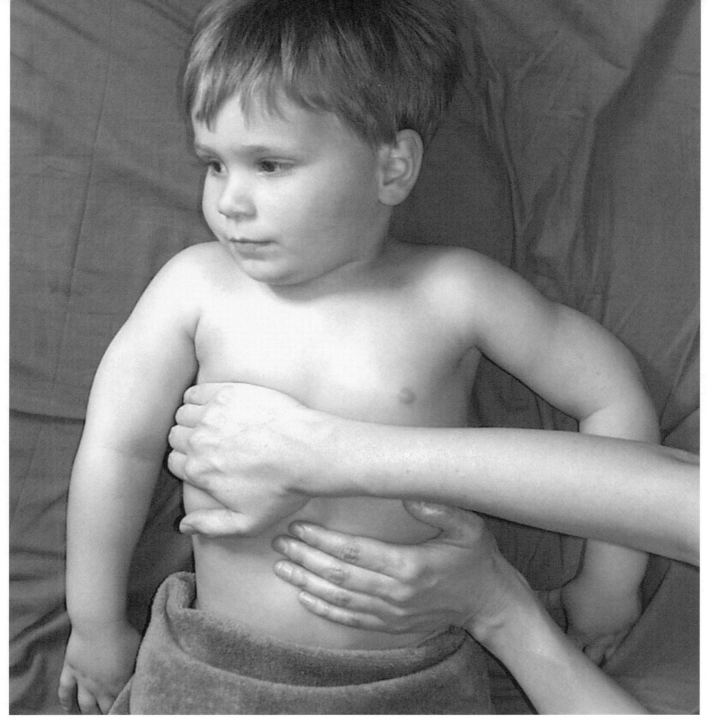

U. Stroke across the chest and abdomen. End by letting your hands rest on the solar plexus.

To perform face massage you can either be seated behind the child or massage the face from the front. In the following segment the giver is positioned behind.

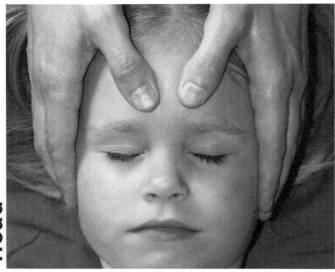

V. Stroke from the middle of the forehead to the temples. Use your thumbs or fingertips.

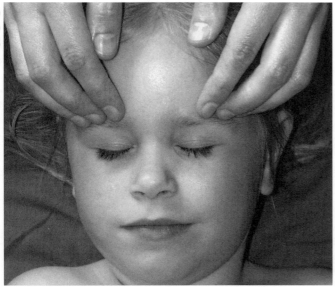

W. Stroke the eyebrows with thumbs or fingertips.

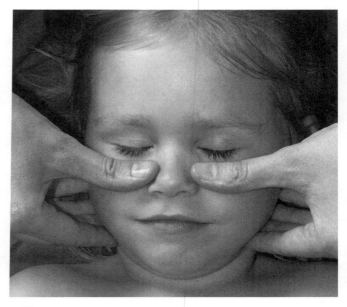

X. Then make circles around the eyes in each direction.

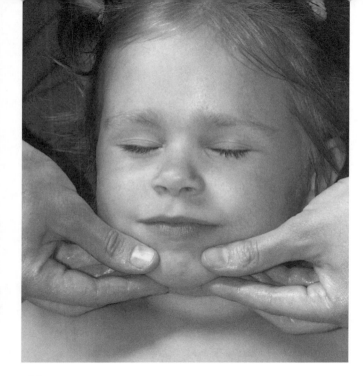

Y. Stroke the jaw from the point of the chin towards the ears and rub the ears and the earlobes.

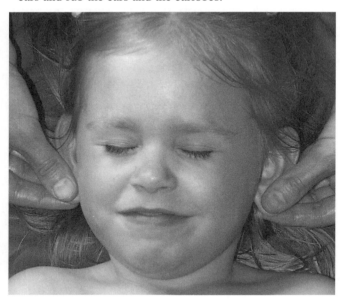

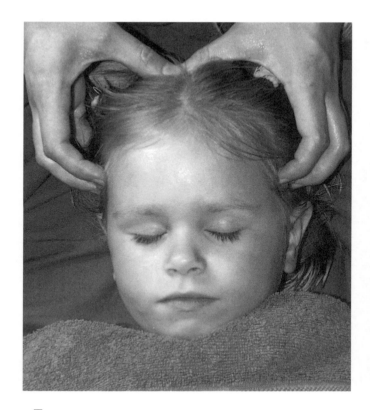

Z. Make circles with your fingertips in the scalp. End by holding the head. Thank the child for being receptive and allowing you to give.

If you want, you can round up with connecting strokes from the top of the head down the arms, side of legs and down to the feet. Hold the feet for a while. Say thank you.

School children

Starting school is a big event for most children. For some, excitement and nervous tension is involved. During such occasions it is a miracle to have a teacher who understands the benefits of touch and massage in creating security. In the USA this is a provocative thought, but in Sweden there are classes from elementary school to junior high, where daily touch is integrated into the teaching. The mode of touch can vary from the teacher consciously holding his or her hand on the shoulder of a student while standing at the student's desk, to the whole class rubbing each other's backs. Where this type of touch has been integrated in the classroom the atmosphere has become much calmer. The communication between the children, as well as between children and teacher, has improved, and a nicer environment for both parties has been created. For the child, as an individual, positive effects, such as easier learning, less stress and increased well being, have resulted.

Kids of all ages normally appreciate School Massage. Even the toughest boys and the worst antagonists are smitten after a while. It does not take long before demands are being made for a break during class-time to have a neck and shoulder massage. It has happened that students ask that massage be incorporated in the schedule, if the teachers have omitted in doing so.

For some, massage becomes something that opens a new door in life. Through a colleague I heard this story about a boy in the third grade. The boy was large for his age and overweight, and most of the time alone. He did not seem to be comfortable with himself and nobody else seemed to enjoy him either. When massage was at first introduced in his class he refused to participate. He stepped aside watching the activities. After a while he found it acceptable to at least give a massage. This became the turning point for the boy. It turned out that he had the loveliest massage hands and soon he was everybody's favorite masseur. The kids stood in line to get massaged by him.

Another story shows how wrong things can go when a child, who has become accustomed to receiving massage at an early age does not continue to get it when starting school. During his pre-school years a boy had received massage on a regular basis. He enjoyed and benefited from the sessions and he seemed to be developing well. However when he started school in the fall the massaging stopped and he suddenly changed. He became restless and fidgety. He became difficult to have in the classroom and the problem was discussed with his parents. Because the boy had not had such problems previously nobody knew what to do about the new situation. After a couple of more months the boy's behavior became so disturbing that the mother had to take him to a psychologist. At the first meeting with the psychologist the little boy burst into tears, exhausted, telling the adults, "But don't you see it is massage that I need!"

This story I think clearly states how clever children are in understanding their own needs and also how important it is to create peace and quiet for the growing body and mind. So if your child is showing signs of having a hard time with school I suggest you help it with tender, loving touch.

Teenagers

"You are born wet, screaming and hungry-
Then everything gets worse."
- Bumper sticker

In puberty a new phase in life is entered. The stage of not being a child and not being a grown up can be frustrating to many. Very few people seem to pass this period in life without problems.

When the hormones are activated the body and mind of the child is changed. These changes sometimes make it difficult for the parents to recognize their child, who used to be happy and balanced. The teenager has an even harder time understanding all the flammable, intense feelings of confusion and hopelessness. The body, which used to be cooperative and agile to be in, suddenly feels clumsy and out of proportion.

Massage can be of help to many teenagers (and their parents). Tactile stimulation as such can help the body to balance the release of hormones. At times it can also be comforting to feel cared for, when otherwise struggling to become independent and strong. If a child is allowed to relax and let go once in a while, it may find the path to maturity a little easier.

If the child is not used to massage, it may not be easy to introduce it at this point. Girls seem by nature to be more open-minded to massage and other kinds of body care. This is probably dependent upon the female's predisposition for care, which correlates to the higher level of Oxytocin hormone in their blood. Males, whether they are teenagers or adults, also possess a natural need for touch. However, the majority of the male population does not find beauty and/or bodycare especially appealing. Girls on the other hand are putting cream and lotion on and massaging with oil, just because it is good for their skin.

I have seen many boys at an early age react with resistance to all activities involving "sticky" substances such as sunscreens or body lotions. For boys, massage has to have a more practical touch. "Football" or "hockey legs" have to be taken care of as well as "tennis arms," "skateboard feet," and "guitar fingers." One has to find an opening which the younger or older boy can accept. This will be the starting point. From this point, body part after body part can be attached to the routine. If the "basketball calves" have received their rub, maybe the back that has carried the back-pack to and from school also has to be massaged, and so on. Before you know it you will be asked when the next massage session is going to take place.

It is worth trying to establish massage as a natural part of the teenager's life. Teenagers do not always allow their parents to continue their endearments of good night hugs and cheek strokes. To many parents it is like a term of grace to be allowed to massage the teenager. Through the hands the parent, can for a moment, share all the tenderness and love he or she feels for the child. When the teenager is dropping hard words, slamming doors and is bewailing their destiny, it might be comforting to know that in spite of everything the parental love and care is still there. Massage will prove that the teenager, in spite of low spirits and caprices, is still lovable.

A woman wrote to me about her thirteen-year-old stepson. She found him quiet and withdrawn, and he did not spend much time interacting with the rest of the family. The woman did not feel accepted by the stepson. She thought they had a poor relationship, which bothered her. After learning tactile massage through continuing education at her work, she started to massage the boy. After just a couple of massages he began to change. On his own accord he began to spend time with the other members of the family. He was more talkative and interactive. The woman felt that through massage she had obtained a tool to show the stepson she cared about him. He, on the other hand, feeling her warmth for him in such a palpable way,

dared to trust her. This meant a lot to both of them.

The increased hormone production in teenagers also leads to their increased interest in the opposite sex. Infatuations, love and attractions will eventually lead to a sexual debut. As sex is infiltrated in most advertisements, music videos, and media, it is easy for a teenager to be misled believing sexual experiences are the key to happiness and success. Society's perception of success is closely related to physical appearance with allusion to sex appeal. Therefore it is easy for young people to believe that sex, even from the very beginning, has to be part of the relationship with the opposite sex.

One often finds that when asking people about their first sexual experience the response is that they think it happened too early, it was not very pleasant, or it took place due to pressure from the outside. Because most people have few tactile experiences, body contact easily becomes the same as sex. One does not know how to be, or how one dares to be, close to somebody without having intercourse. I believe that incorporating massage and touch into a child's up-bringing helps form the foundation for personal security and safety. This, in turn, becomes the basis to broadening the repertoire of how we as human beings, in a physical sense, are interacting with each other. There is a broad spectrum of touch between hand-shaking and "love-making." It is a gift to experience the full width of touch; everything from the motherly/fatherly care, the touch among family members and friends, to the sensual caressing between lovers, to finally the sexual touch experience with a partner. When it comes down to it, it is really the warmth and closeness of another human being that makes us feel good about ourselves. Sex just becomes an extra bonus in intimate relationships.

A teenager that has been brought up with displays of affection through loving touch, and whose body has been looked upon as perfect and beautiful, will most likely have a positive outlook towards his/her own body. Unfortunately though, all too many find that the teenage years are filled with self-denial and bodily complexes.

Many youngsters today find food, eating habits, weight-management and body shape difficult subjects to deal with. When it comes to the shape and size of our bodies, we are exposed to a "media indoctrination" which is stronger than ever. The overwhelming message about the skinny ideal may be hard to resist for a teenager. Eating disorders are not uncommonly the result. The problems of eating disorders are complex, and are partly due to the fashion industry and the physical ideals of modern society. Eating disorders tend to increase among young people and make life difficult to many, mentally as well as physically.

What can be done to help these adolescent children toward a healthier and more balanced relationship with their bodies? Studies made in the U.S.A. on adolescent children with Anorexia Nervosa and Bulimia have shown that massage can work as a tool and complement in the treatment of these eating disorders. Regular massage treatments during a five-week period improved the participants' bodily awareness, and the symptoms of mental depression and anxiety decreased. Significant decreases in the level of stress hormones in their bodies were also noted.

To have one teenager with an eating disorder in the family can be tough for all family members. It commonly affects every family member in one way or another. To have both the afflicted party and the other family members give and receive conscious and loving touch may perhaps not completely eliminate the problem, but can somehow supply the nourishment for the love and acknowledgement from which healing may arise.

Touch for a more peaceful world

"Massage instead of massacre"

Massage and touch can be looked upon as a resource for making peace. In cultures where children receive an abundance of loving touch the violence among adults is less. Researcher Tiffany Field, Ph.D., of the Touch Research Institute in Miami, believes that lack of affectionate touching may be linked to male violence. In a cross-cultural study it was found that French pre-schoolers touched each other twice as much during play as did kids in the United States. The French children rarely acted aggressively whereas the American children were aggressive 29 percent of the time. Interestingly, France among other high-touch societies, shows low rates of adult violence in comparison to the United States, which tops the homicide rates of all developed countries.

Based on the theory of touch induced peace, some special schools in Sweden are working with violent, and so-called maladjusted, youngsters. These young people are taught massage, theoretically as well as practically, during a nine-week education session. Many of the teenage participants, who are in this program voluntarily, undergo changes during this period. Altered states of behavior are noted among the teenagers. Their protective and closed manners change to more open attitudes, displayed through increased communication and a tendency toward calmer physical contact. One of the participants, who used to be a gang member, expressed it in a colorful way saying, "It is cool to be okay."

For some, the massage classes have totally transformed their lives. These young people have begun to experience an appetite for studying and have gained a new understanding of life setting goals. With newfound self-confidence they have gone on to take classes at an established and well-known massage school where they have earned diplomas as masseurs.

The plant's bright blessings spring forth
From earth's gentle being,
And human children rise up
With grateful hearts to join
The spirits of the world.

- Rudolf Steiner

Buddy Massage – When – Where – How?

Children who are accustomed to touch and massage may want to massage each other. Buddy Massage is primarily meant to be a seated massage that is easy to do on siblings, playmates and friends. Three variants of Buddy Massage will be presented; a short seated routine, a longer seated routine, and an ordinary reclining massage with clothes on. Buddy Massage can be a helping tool in training and fostering children to respectfully touch each other. The concept includes massage taught to the adults for children as well as techniques for children to use in massaging each other. A prerequisite is that the adult has first acquired the practical and theoretical knowledge about massage. Buddy Massage should be so simple that it can easily be performed anywhere at home, or included in the school agenda without disturbing other activities.

Naturally, Child Massage can be used as a complement to

Buddy Massage, and adjusted to the situation. My thought though, is that when the child has started school, clothes-off massages are preferably done in a home environment among family members.

When to do Buddy Massage

Buddy Massage may be well suited whenever the children feel like massaging, or one wants to influence the atmosphere in a group of kids, whether it be in a classroom or a play-ground. As always, it is up to the children whether or not they choose to participate. They always have the right to decide over their own body when it comes to touching and massage.

When not to use Buddy Massage

Buddy Massage should not be used to heal an injury which has not first been examined by medically trained and licensed personnel.

Where to do Buddy Massage

Children can perform Buddy Massage at home, at pre-school, at school, at the youth club or in their sports team.

How to prepare for Buddy Massage

Few practical preparations are needed for Buddy Massage. A chair or stool, or some cushions on the floor will do as equip-ment. The only thing the children must do is ask their friend for permission to massage. It can also be an advantage to be in a peaceful place.

If a tape recorder is available, it might be a good idea to play some relaxing music. The right kind of music can create a peaceful and harmonious atmosphere.

How to teach Buddy Massage to the children

Small children can be introduced to Buddy Massage through a massage fairy tale. The adult tells and shows. To begin with, only a few strokes are taught and then more and more are added following each massage time. For older children simple show-look-imitate teaching techniques function well.

**Buddy Massage from
A to Z**

Following are three suggestions of how you can work with Buddy Massage. The first one is a short seated massage routine for shoulders, neck and head. It will take no more than five minutes to do. If you want a longer version with arm and back massage added the second routine might be chosen. The longer seated massage can take anywhere from ten to twenty minutes depending on how much time is given to each movement.

The lying down full body routine finishes the "Alphabet of Buddy Massage." This variant can easily be done after physical education and sports wherever there is space to lie down. Some of the massage moves are repeated in different variations. Others appear only once. You can use all the different moves freely making your own version of seated or reclining Buddy Massage. The following is only a suggestion for simple basic moves. Every person, furthermore, has their own arsenal of moves so the possibilities for development are eternal. My philosophy is that "whatever feels right is right." The actual technique has no prominent position in Buddy Massage. The most important part is that the heart is there and that the children are training their empathetic skills.

Ask the children to pair up. The receiver of massage sits on the floor or on a chair. The giver stands behind them. If the receiver finds it more comfortable he or she may lean against a table with the forehead resting on the arms. Ask the giver to ask the buddy if he or she wants massage. If the answer is "yes," the giver will put his/her hand on the shoulders of the receiver. Both take a deep breath and relax. The receiver may close their eyes.

Ask the children to keep contact with the buddy throughout the massage. This is important in creating continuity. If the massage is too interrupted and not flowing the receiver will find it hard to relax.

The children need to know beforehand that massage should feel good and should not hurt. It is important that the kids are sensitive to each other. One should stress the fact that it is the receiver who decides what feels good and what does not.

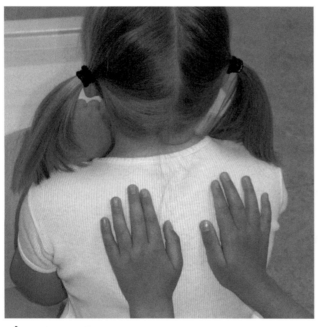

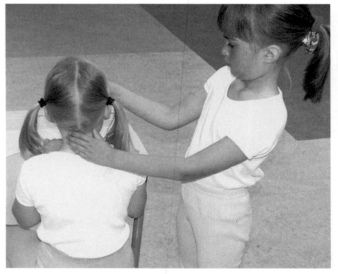

A. "Glasses"

Make circular strokes around the shoulder blades. Stroke with cupped hands from the top of the shoulders to the sides. Flatten the hands and continue around the shoulder blades. Let the hands meet at the middle of the back and glide up to the top of the shoulders. Repeat.

B. "Rabbit Grip"

Stand beside the receiver and support his/her head with one hand on the forehead (unless the receiver is leaning against the desk). Take a "rabbit grip" in the neck and knead softly with fingers on one side of the neck and thumb on the other side. Caution! Do not press too far forward toward the throat.

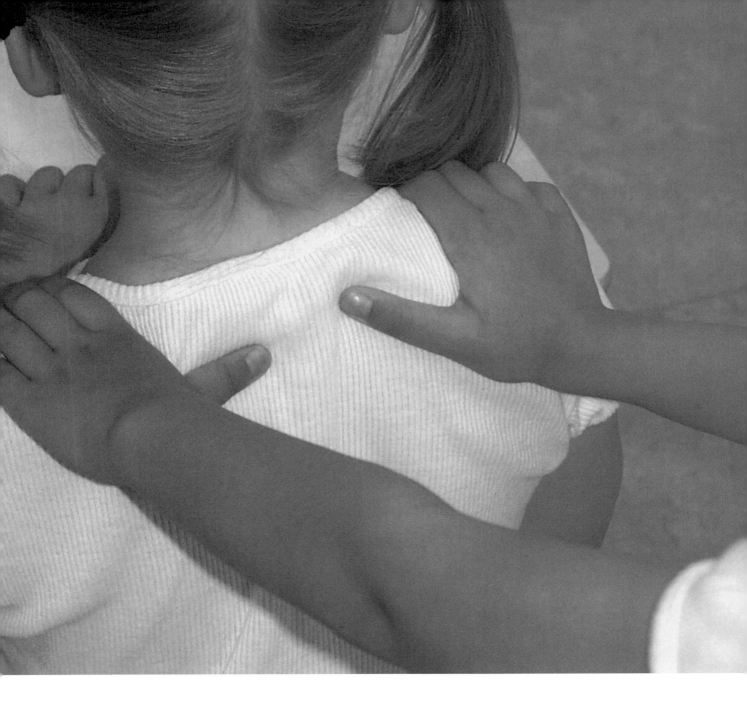

C. "Kneading"
Put the hands on the top of the shoulder and knead the soft tissue with palms and fingers.

D. "Hairdresser's fingertips"

Let the fingers glide like a comb through the hair. Make circles with the fingertips in the scalp.

E. "Slide"

Stroke from the head down the side of the neck and shoulders.

End the session by holding the hands still on top of the shoulders for a moment. Have the children thank each other for giving and receiving.

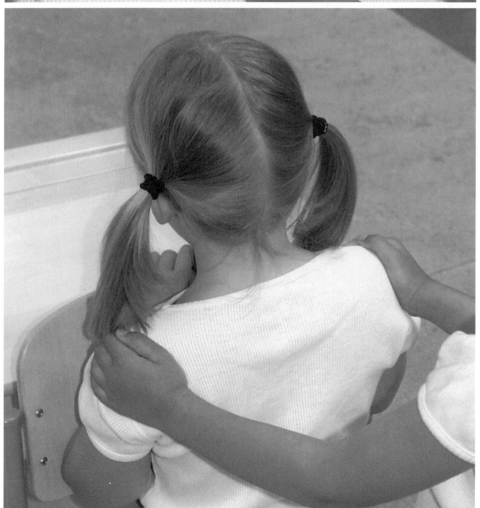

101

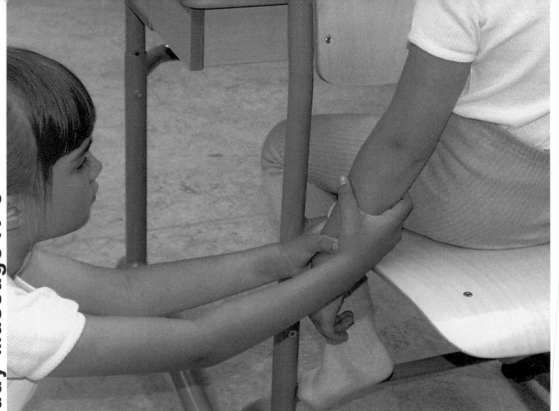

In this version the child should straddle the chair and turn towards the backrest. The receiver needs to turn the chair so that the back will be easily accessible for the giver. All the previous moves from A to E are done first and then follows:

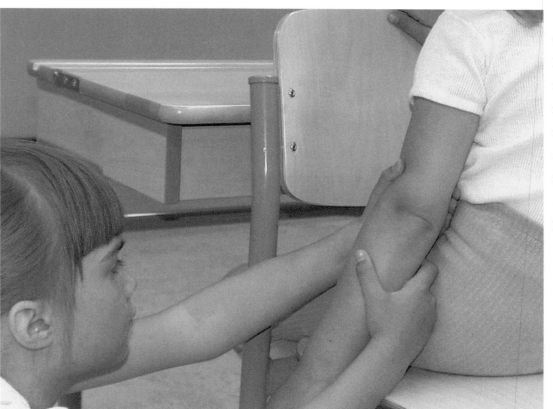

F **"Rope climbing"**

Grab the arm with one hand on each side. The receiver should try to relax the arm. Start right below the armpit and press gently and firmly up and down the arm. Grab and press the hand.

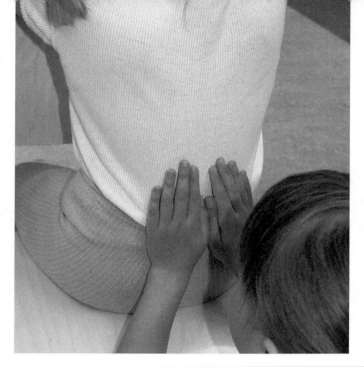

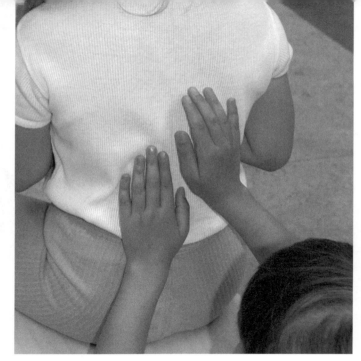

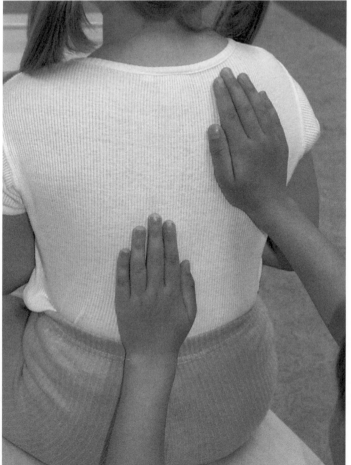

G. "T-stroke"

Stand behind the receiver again. Put the hands on the lower back and make a wide stroke on the back and across the shoulders. Draw a T. Glide down the sides and repeat.

H. "Bear walk"

Put the hands on each side of the spine. Start at the lower back and alternately press with the heels of the hands. Move slowly and heavily upwards, like a bear walking. Relax the fingers and swing the body to get a nice rhythm. When you reach the neck, walk down again.

I. "Scrubbing"

Start with the hands on each side of the spine. Rub the hands briskly up and down. Work the whole back.

J. "Cat stroke"

Stroke with full hand down the back. Let one hand follow the other. Stroke "with the furs" over the whole back. Finish by stroking lightly from the top of the head down the arms and down the back.

Let the hands rest on the shoulders for a short moment. Thank each other.

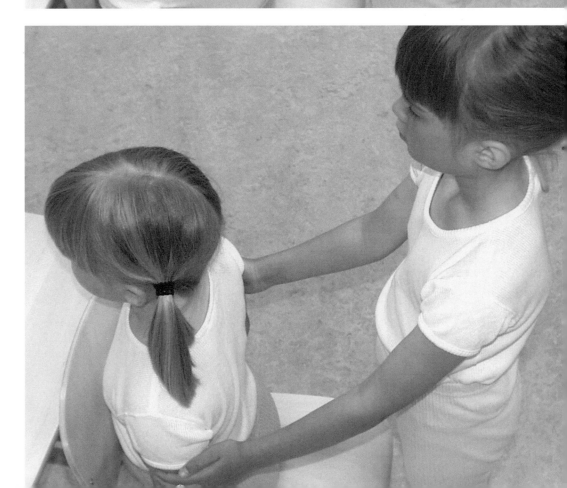

The receiver lies prone on a sleeping pad, sport mat, soft carpet, etc. The giver kneels beside the buddy. Both take a couple of deep breaths and relax. The giver calmly puts the hands on the lower back. Remind the children to keep contact with their buddies at all times. Only soft tissue should be massaged and the receiver is asked to object as soon as anything feels uncomfortable.

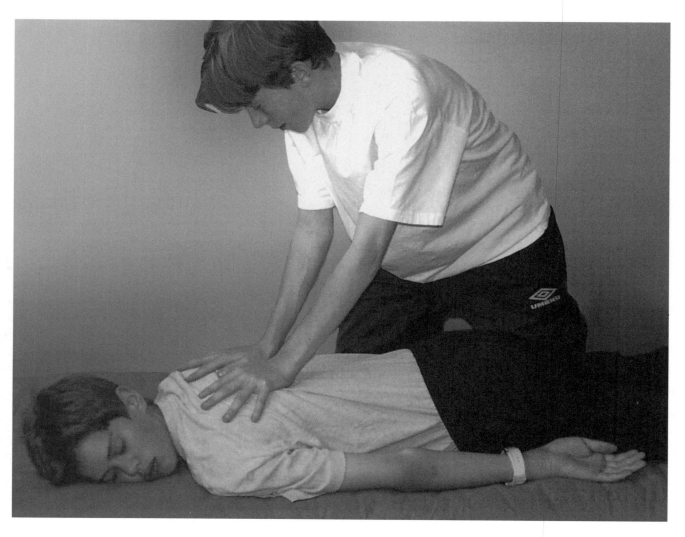

K   **"Swim stroke"**
Stroke the back with swim-like movements. Start at the backbone and "swim" up the whole back. Make large and/or small "Swim strokes."

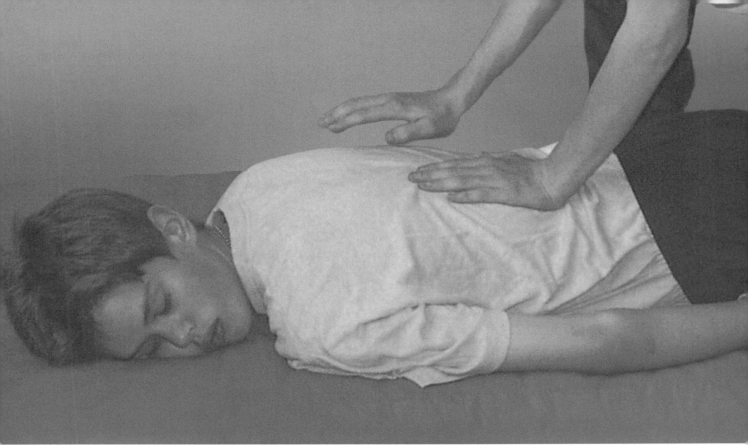

L.

"Bear walk on the back"

Walk up the back with one hand on each side of the spine. The pressure is on the heel of the hand but the whole hand touches. Sway from side to side in a calm, nice rhythm as you walk. Caution! Do not press on bony parts or anything that is not soft.

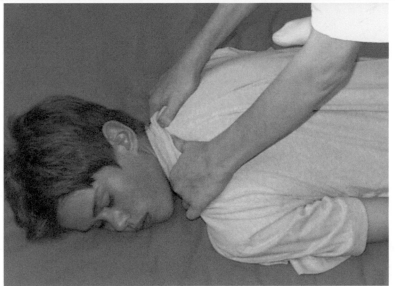

M. **"Kneading"**

Take a friendly grip of the top of the shoulders with one hand on each side. Press and knead lightly with fingers and heels of hands.

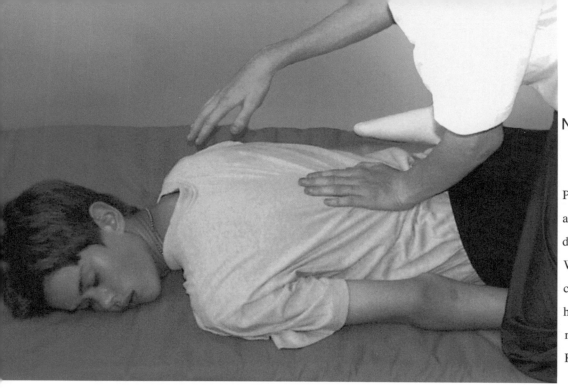

N. "Cat strokes on back and legs"

Place a hand at the neck and stroke all the way down to the buttocks. When the first hand has come down the other hand starts from the neck making a similar stroke. Repeat.

Then make strokes down the legs. Let one hand follow the other. Work one leg at a time.

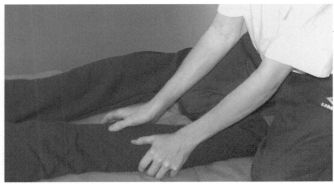

O. "Bear walk on legs"

Start above the Achilles tendon with one hand on each side of the leg. Walk slowly up the leg with even pressure. Avoid the back of the knee. Work up to the sitting bone and down again. Repeat the other leg.

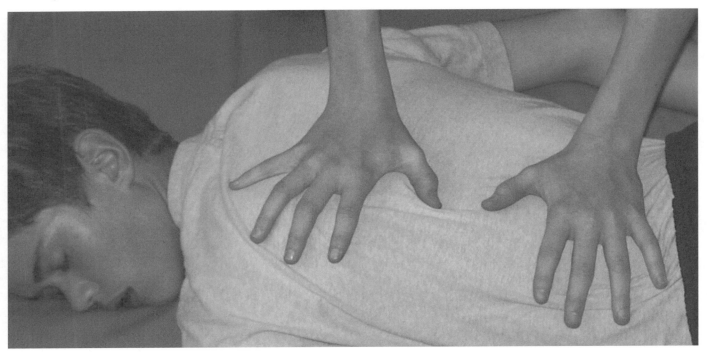

P. "Rock the boat"

Rock one leg at a time. The receiver should try to relax as much as possible. Glide with the hands on the back and rock the torso.

When the rocking is finished make a connecting stroke from the top of the head down to the heels. Keep the hands on the heels for a while before the buddy is asked to turn over.

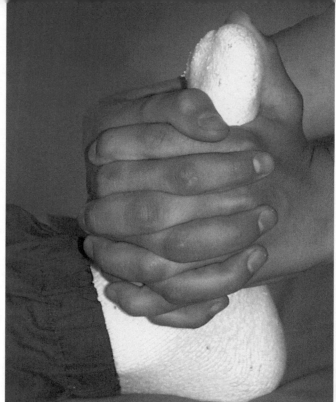

Q. "Foot prayer"

The receiver is lying on the back. Clasp the hands around the buddy's foot. Rub the foot between the hands.

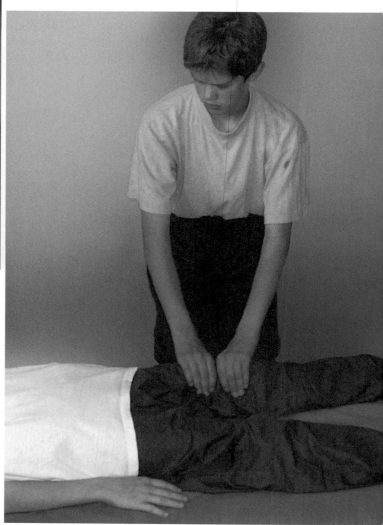

R. "Rabbit grip on thigh"

Place the hands next to each other on the thigh. Press gently and lift simultaneously. Work with the hands alternating.

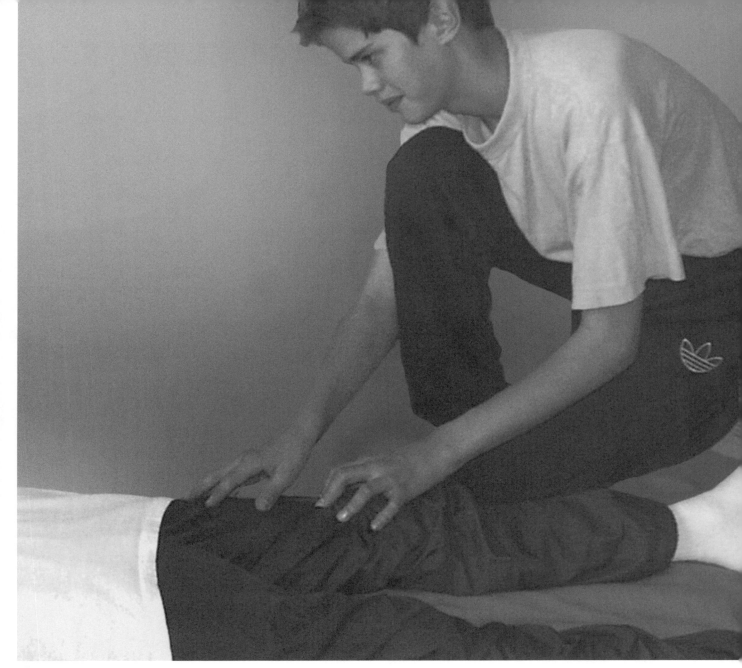

S. "Feather strokes on leg"

Stroke with fingertips in short motions from the thigh to the

foot. End by holding the foot.

Repeat from **Q** to **S** on the other leg.

Make connecting strokes on both legs simultaneously.

Stroke from the hipbones down to toes.

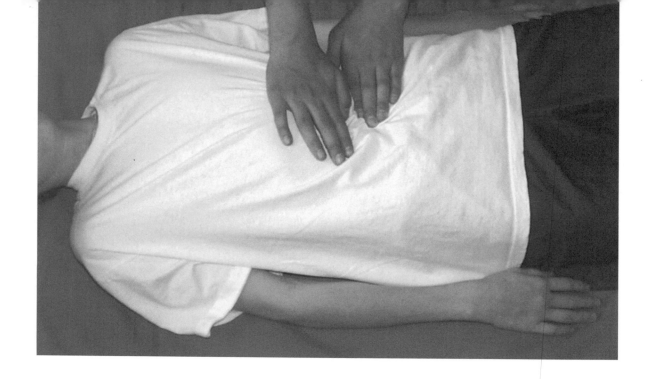

T. "Stomach-clock"

Gently put the hands on the Abdomen. Imagine the hands of a clock moving from the navel. Stroke lightly clockwise on the abdomen.

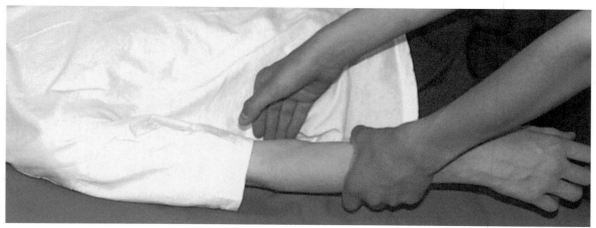

U. "Rope climbing"

Grab an arm with both hands. Start at the wrist and "climb" up the arm with one hand over the other. "Climb" down again.

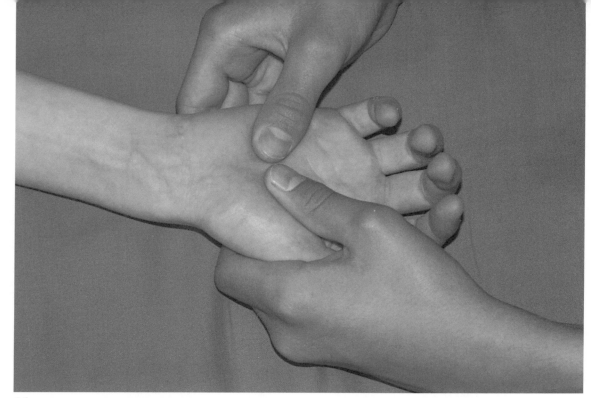

V. "Thumb walk in the palm"

Support the hand of the buddy and press with thumbs in the palm.

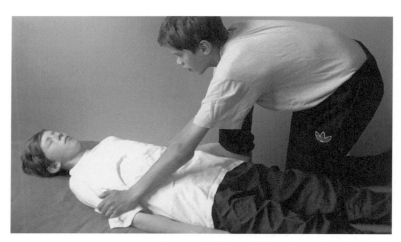

W. "Feather strokes on arm"

Make short strokes with fingertips from shoulder to hand.

Repeat **U**, **V** and **W** on the other side. Make connecting strokes on both arms simultaneously from shoulders to fingertips.

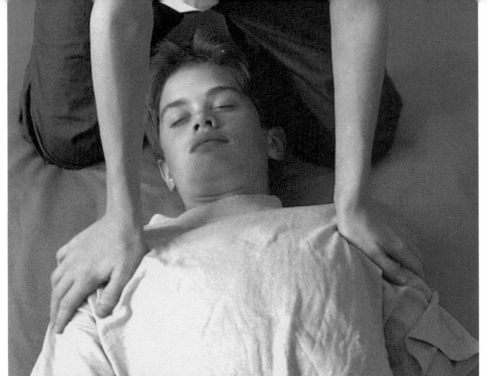

X. "Cat steps on shoulders"

Sit at the head and cup the hands on the shoulders. Press gently one shoulder at a time. Alternate.

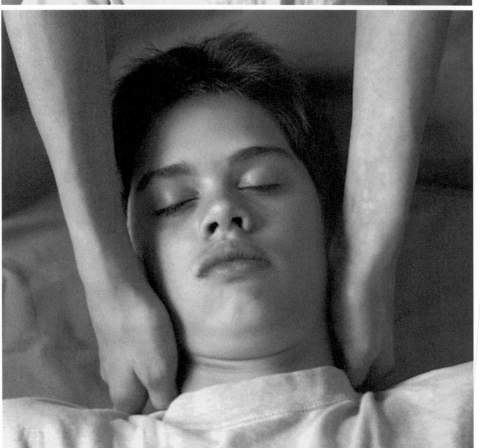

Y. "Neck circles"

Sit at the head. Push the fingers under the neck till they meet. Make light circles on the soft tissue of the neck.

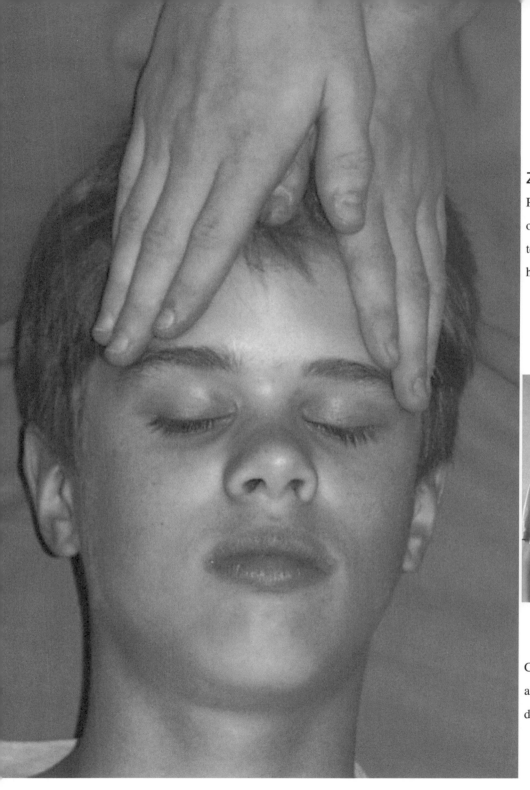

Z. "No worries"

Place the fingers on the middle of the forehead. Stroke to the temples. End by holding the head for a while.

Carefully take the hands away and ask the receiver to take a deep breath and wake up.

Reactions to massage and touch

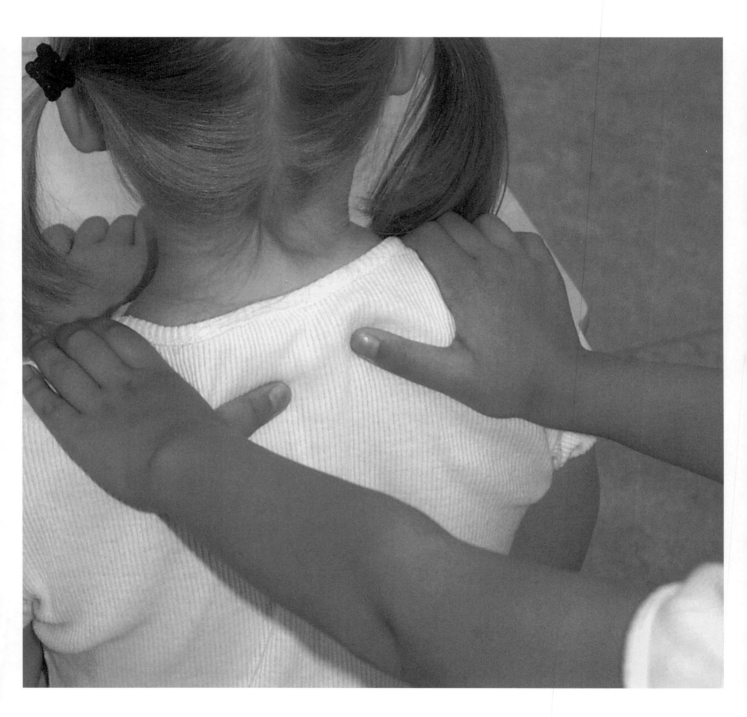

Most people seem to agree that touch and massage is pleasant. Many wonder how something that is "only" pleasant can really have a deeper effect on the body and soul. To assist in answering that question we shall take a closer look at the skin that we touch, the nervous system which responds to touch, and the physiological reactions released by touch.

The Skin

The skin is seldom looked at as an organ, but that is exactly what it is. It is actually the largest organ of the body. The skin of an adult measures 17-20 square feet. The skin's structure is complex and highly specialized, which can be expected considering it is the largest border between the body and its surroundings. Microscopically the skin is formed in an intimate unification of two distinct tissues: the epidermis and dermis. Furthermore a third, deeper layer is usually included – the hypodermis. It is due to this structure that the skin is such an efficient protection against dehydration and mechanical and chemical injuries.

The skin limits and regulates the body's temperature depending on our need for keeping warm or cooling down. This regulation is done through the opening and closure of the pores, which enables the secretion of sweat and waste products. Thus, the skin is an organ of secretion and at the same time also an organ of absorption. This means that the skin, so to speak, "eats" or "takes in" whatever is put on it, which is why it can, for instance, be used for medication purposes. The skin also serves as a blood reserve, as well as a producer of vitamin D and melanin.

Included in the composition of "skin," is the mucous membrane, which functions as an inner skin. The skin is surrounding the whole organism. The surface of the skin continues over the lips and goes on in the form of the mucous membrane in the oral cavity, throat, esophagus, stomach, and intestines, until it meets the outer skin again at the anus. The mucous membrane continues inside the urethra, covering the walls of the bladder and the urethra, all the way to the kidneys. In men, the walls of the spermatic cord up to the testicles are covered by mucous membrane, and in women the vagina, uterus, and uterine tubes are covered. The skin is embracing us from the outside and the mucous membrane, is creating an inner "skin surface" on the inside.

Both skin and mucous membranes communicate with the brain via tiny receptors. There are many different kinds of receptors, each kind having its own structure and function. There are receptors reacting to touch, pressure, heat, vibration, cold, tickling, and pain. When for example the touch receptors in the skin register touch, signals travel to the brain via nerve pathways and we become aware of sensing touch. In certain places on the body very little stimuli is needed before we sense touch, in other places it takes more. It depends on how close the receptors lie in the skin. There are normally 1000-5000 of the different receptors per square centimeter, or approximately 1600-9000 per square inch. The receptors are closest in the palm of the hand, on the fingertips, lips and on the tip of the toes.

The Nervous System

The nervous system can be considered an electrical system of the body, where messages travel from one part of the body to another. The brain and the spinal cord are called the central nervous system (CNS), and among other functions are responsible for receiving information and organizing reflexes. The CNS is in charge of learning and memory, as well as, of planning and executing voluntary movements. A network of nerves extends from the brain and the spinal cord going out to the whole body, which is known as the peripheral nervous system (PNS). This particular nervous system creates the conditions for exchange of information between the internal and external environment and the brain.

The peripheral nervous system is divided into two parts. One part, known as the somatic nervous system, transmits messages about voluntary activities. It handles all the body movements we do voluntarily. The other part of the peripheral nervous system cannot directly be influenced by will power (the autonomic nervous system). This portion of the system refers to the functions that work automatically, such as digestion and breathing. Let us look a little closer at the latter, the autonomic (independent) nervous system.

The autonomic nervous system again is divided into functional systems. We can call one part a stress system (the sympathetic nervous system) and the other part a relaxation system (the parasympathetic nervous system). These two are similar to a balancing scale. To feel well we need both sides to balance equally.

One can, in a way, attribute the survival of human beings on earth to the stress system. In the beginning of human history the cavemen had to defend themselves against intruders and predators to survive. The sympathetic nervous system prepares the body to manage life-threatening situations. Let us imagine that an angry bear is attacking a caveman in the forest. To save his own life he needs either to quickly flee or to try to kill the bear. To manage this the body switches on the stress system, which prepares it for fight or flight. The blood circulation and pulse increases, the pumping of the heart gets stronger, blood vessels in the skin and inner organs constrict so that the blood pressure increases. The blood vessels of the active muscles dilate so that the muscles can work better. The liver glycogen is split and released as blood sugar, which is fuel to the muscles. Digestion is put on hold. In a stress or crisis situation the body does not give digestion priority. Additionally we can see how the pupils of the caveman are widening, he is sweating, his hair is raising and he breathes rapidly. All these signs and reactions are necessary for him to have a chance to defend himself against the life threatening situation the attacking bear represents. Thanks to the ability of the body to react this way we can perform better than we think is possible. In our small example with the caveman he manages to run away from the bear and so he survives.

The sympathetic nervous system works well even in modern man. Nowadays there are usually no bears to run from so the stress situations look a little different. Real and sometimes imagined threats and their consequences, such as poor economy, unemployment, too much work, an unpleasant working atmosphere, rocky relationships, and so on, cause the stress system to switch on. In children, stress can occur due to separation, punishment, high expectations, loneliness, and mobbing. Unfortunately much of modern stress poses situations from which we cannot run or fight back. This can lead to the sympathetic nervous system keeping the body in a constant grip of alarm. In the long run, this state can cause high blood pressure, muscle pain, bad digestion, disturbed sleep, diarrhea, constipation, and tiredness, just to list a few stress-related symptoms.

In comparison to the caveman, who could, as soon as the danger was over, calm down in the cave among supporting members of the clan, modern man tends to get stuck in the stress trap, and therefore deters the natural regulation of the body from taking place. However, nature's wisdom has prevailed again, and has provided a system to re-create the balance in the body. The anti-stress system slows down the heart rate, constricts the pupils, increases peristalsis and at the same time increases the secretion of bile and insulin in the digestive system. The blood pressure is balanced and the breathing calms down, while salivation increases and muscle tone decreases.

To obtain the balancing mechanism, most people need to have the parasympathetic nervous system stimulated. An effective way to start anti-stress reactions in the body is through touch. Of course we have unconsciously discovered that. Most people develop small tactile tricks to calm themselves with. Some stroke the forehead; another wrings the hands, crosses the arms, wets the lips or twists the hair. Remembering that the mucous membrane functions the same way as the skin. Stimulation of the mucous membrane will bring about similar effects of relaxation and peacefulness. This occurs when we eat or drink. Many people calm their anxiety and worries through touching themselves on the inside, or in other words, they eat or drink themselves to a state of relaxation.

Receptors for touch, pressure, vibration, and heat are connected to the parasympathetic nervous system. Through the stimulation of these receptors the anti-stress system can be activated and the body can balance the effects of stress. Therefore, massage, touch, hot baths, big hugs and long embraces are a must in a world where "bears" are not always visible.

Reactions to Touch

There are pure physiological explanations to why touch creates well being. Neuro -physiologists have found that there are special kinds of chemical messengers, peptides, in the nervous system. The peptides are made of amino acids and their first task is to transmit information from one cell to another. Soft touch, for example, activates parasympathetic reactions and influences different pleasure centers in the brain. In both cases peptides function as transmitters. The peptides are also widely stimulating the parasympathetic nervous system and therefore increasing physical and mental well being. The earliest acknowledged group of peptides is the endorphins of the brain. Endorphin is a morphine-like substance made by the body itself. It is commonly known as "happiness hormones" because of the effects it has on the human creature. Now it has been seen that another peptide, Oxytocin, has similar effects.

Oxytocin, also called the "peace-and-calm-hormone," is both a hormone and a neurotransmitter. Historically, Oxytocin has been known mostly as a hormone released in women during labor and breast-feeding. New knowledge teaches us that Oxytocin is present in both men and women and is causing much more than uterine contractions and milk ejec-

tion. Most research on Oxytocin has been performed on rats but researchers have reason to believe Oxytocin has similar effects on the human. The "peace-and-calm-hormone" has shown to produce:

Decreased muscle tension

For a muscle to function at an optimal level it needs sufficient circulation and blood supply. When tension occurs in a muscle the circulation is partially strangled. The inflow of new oxygenated blood and nutrients, which are necessary for the muscle to work, are decreased simultaneously as the level of toxins and waste products increase making it harder for the muscle to do its job. Fatigue is a result and in the long run muscle pain and ache can occur. Relaxed muscles are stronger and more endurable giving the body a broader range of motion. Since touch releases Oxytocin, massage can be a very powerful method to decrease tension in the muscles.

Higher pain threshold

Pain engages the sympathetic nervous system and puts the body in a state of alarm. When in pain our fight-or-flight-behavior is activated so that we can escape from the danger. If we pinch a finger, experience growing pains, or if it is teething or colic that hit us, the pain can be soothed by touch. There is a built-in response of wanting to touch, blow on, or hold the aching spot. The body knows automatically that it will help. If the level of Oxytocin is high in the body it is less sensitive to pain. That means the same "amount" of pain is not felt as strongly as usual. A higher pain threshold shows in less experience of pain.

Better digestion and nutritional absorption

The vagus nerve, which is connected to the heart, lungs and stomach, is stimulated by Oxytocin. Oxytocin decreases the intake of food for a few hours but will, over a longer period of time, have a stimulating effect on the appetite. High levels of Oxytocin increase the digestive activity. When digestion is working efficiently the levels of other effecting hormones are influenced as well. The appetite improves and weight gain will follow. Oxytocin stimulates the stomach, the intestines–the part of the metabolism that stores nutrients, thereby insuring that nutrients are absorbed more sufficiently and extra energy is stored in the body. Research has shown that women who have higher levels of Oxytocin, are giving birth to bigger babies, and that babies with poor growth will gain weight if they are touched more.

Proof to increased digestive activity is hearing the stomach making sounds while being massaged or stroked.

Lower pulse and blood pressure

Both pulse and blood pressure are influenced by the lower activity in the sympathetic nervous system caused by Oxy-

tocin. The heart rate is slowed down so that pulse and blood pressure can normalize. The calming effect of Oxytocin can be felt if someone holds or strokes you when you are scared or upset, or when you take a hot bath after a busy day.

Less aggression and greater calmness

Aggression can be seen as a waste product to the fight-or-flight-behavior of the stress system. With increased levels of Oxytocin in the body the preparation for fight will be neutralized and calmness can rule both body and mind. When the touch receptors are stimulated the brain releases Oxytocin. Both the hands of the giver as well as the skin of the receiver send signals about touch to the central nervous system. This means both persons will experience the calming effects of Oxytocin. One example of how this works is elderly people who often become low and depressed due to isolation. When they get a dog or a cat as company they become calmer and happier. Through petting and stroking the pet, Oxytocin is released, which contributes to the change in mood. Of course the pet too, also feels better when scratched and petted! The same mechanism can be seen in aggressive children who experience staying in the countryside among animals, or perhaps get a pet of their own. Tactile contact between animals and children creates peace and can result in less aggression. These reactions occur between people as well. It is known that in cultures where people touch, aggressive behavior is less likely to be present. Women, who generally have higher levels of Oxytocin than men, are considered to be less aggressive. One could call Oxytocin a "peace hormone." Maybe the world would look different if those in power were given an extra dosage of the "peace hormone" before entering important meetings and negotiations!

Revoked fear

Fear serves us for short moments when we need to achieve something extra. We are more alert, we run faster and defend ourselves more if we are afraid. If the fear is too overpowering it may in some cases even paralyze us. Fear fills its purpose when it counts, when the threat is really there. On the other hand, fear can be seen more as a slave driver than a helper. An under-lying fear of not being able to manage or cope, of becoming abused or punished, or of getting expelled or rejected, can stress the body to the extent that one's health is undermined and peace of mind disturbed. Touch-released Oxytocin revokes the fear and has the same effect on the body as Valium. Therefore, closeness and warm touch can help chase the ghosts of fear away.

Increased curiosity and communication and better bonding to others

It has been found that curiosity and exploratory traits increase in rats injected with Oxytocin. In humans, similar

behavior has been observed after a period of intermittent touch. Babies who have previously not wanted to have eye contact and seemed apathetic, have sought eye contact and started smiling. Children who have been shy and hard to reach have started to talk and play with other children, and adults who have been in a depressive state of mind begin to bloom and show appreciation for life. Oxytocin seems to help people establish a sense of belonging and reassures them of being accepted by others. A child's perception of how much it is touched is linked to its self-esteem and feeling of worth. Touch creates channels of communication between human beings and the world. Massage builds bridges between people.

As we have seen, Oxytocin clearly plays an important role regarding physical and behavioral aspects. If one recognizes that the substance influences human interaction in a positive way, as well as supports anti-stress effects in the body, then one can conclude that activities that increase Oxytocin in the blood can be used as therapy. This would include bodywork such as massage, various tactile techniques, hot baths, heat treatments, and wraps.

Increased bonding to children and partner

Oxytocin has been seen as an influencing factor in how the mother acts toward her baby. Maternal behavior as we know it, with all the caring and puttering it comes with, is strength-

125

ened with increased Oxytocin levels. The desire to take care of and nurture one's child is taken for granted, but actually can be expressed to various degrees depending on the levels of Oxytocin in the mother. The bonding between mother and child is made easier if the two can be close to each other the first hour after delivery when the mother's body automatically has extra high levels of Oxytocin. Although little research has been made regarding the bonding between father and child, one should discover stronger bonding with increased body contact, through which his blood level of Oxytocin is also increased.

Additionally, it has been seen that Oxytocin plays a role in the formation of heterosexual relationships. The substance has shown to facilitate sexual behavior and bonding between partners in rats. The more Oxytocin the easier it seems to build a monogamous relationship.

If we create a scenario from a family perspective, it would obviously not be enough for the parents to bond with the children and the parents with each other. The kids, too, need to have solidarity with one another. Children, who are richly touched by the parents, have higher levels of Oxytocin, which, therefore, increases the likelihood that bonding will occur even between siblings. Kids with healthy Oxytocin levels are more likely to care for each other, which will complete the Oxytocin circle and make it start feeding itself. With this knowledge in mind, a piece of advice for families would be:

"As often as you can, use caring hands and touch. For ever it will make you love your family so much."

There are also other reactions to touch that might be interesting to mention.

Stronger immune system

It appears that touch can strengthen the immune system. It is known that stress lowers the immune defense, and surely it seems like flu and infections more often hit those who have had too much to do, than with those who have slept well, eaten well and had time to take care of themselves. In studies of HIV-positive persons it was shown that the count of natural killer cells increased after a month of regular massage (45 minutes five times weekly). This indicates that touch has positive effects on the immune system.

Deeper breathing

Furthermore, we can observe that breathing is effected by touching. Natural breathing engages the whole body. Observe an infant asleep, the breathing can be discerned from the fontanel to the feet. Most of us experience, at one time or another in life, tensions in the largest breathing muscle, the diaphragm. Tensions in the diaphragm can effect other parts of the body, among other things causing back pain, constipation, and fatigue.

The diaphragm participates in abdominal breathing. You know it is working well when the belly pushes out as you breathe in. Abdominal breathing is the filtration of larger parts of the lungs with oxygenic air, which thereafter distributes increased amounts of oxygen to the whole body. Each cell in the body is depending on oxygen; therefore it is of great importance that we breathe efficiently.   Unfortunately the majority of people are unaware of the natural breathing pattern and use shallow breathing. The upper parts of the lungs are used but one misses to fill the lower parts of the lungs with air.

During periods of touching, breathing is effected and becomes deeper and calmer. Often the person may take a deep breath and sigh when, so to speak, the transition is made from shallow to deeper breathing. Breathing properly is important to the lungs as organs, but even more so to our physical well being which is dependent on the amount of oxygen available. Deep, calm breathing is a pillar to good health.

Increased elimination

When the body is suffering from stress, the colon is one of the areas effected. That resulting symptom is diarrhea or constipation.

The vagus nerve can be effected by performance agony and nervousness resulting in loose stools. Usually it passes as soon as we have accomplished or managed whatever we were afraid of doing. However, if we do not succeed what we wanted, or were expected to do, the diarrhea might become long term and have a negative impact on our well being.

The calming effects of touch can be used to help a nervous stomach and loose stools. One example of nervous stomachs can be seen in children, especially in girls in the early school years. When the changes from preschool to school are too big and hard to handle, children become stressed. It is not unusual that students also experience the symptoms of stomachache and diarrhea before a test or perhaps when mobbing occurs, or when changing to a new class or school.

A mother I knew massaged the abdomens of her children as soon as something upsetting or stressful did happened to them. She also used massage as a preventive action. She found it helped her children to relax and to regain the peace and harmony in their bodies and souls.

People living under stressful conditions sometimes may not have time to go to the bathroom when they receive signals for bowel movements. If this is repeated frequently it will be interpreted as a signal to remain quiet, and will eventually disappear. Constipation will be the natural consequence. The elimination of waste products is a very important function of the body and should not be neglected. An intestine full of stool will have a severe effect on the body and eventually poison it with other symptoms. Thus, to maintain good health and to avoid constipation, the physical signals of elimination should be obeyed immediately.

Another reason for constipation can be the actual decrease of intestinal movements and this again appears in states of stress. We know the sympathetic nervous system slows down the intestinal activity. If you are leading a stressful life, or you have problems that you find hard to solve, the stress-system can slow the activity of the large intestine down, resulting in constipation. The function of the colon is, among other things, to absorb fluid from the intestinal content before elimination. If the intestinal content is held too long in the colon the stool will dry out making it hard to pass. Everyone who has been constipated, or those who have seen a baby in tears struggling to make a result in the "potty," will realize nature must have wanted this procedure to be less painful. A healthy bowel is emptying soft, well-formed stool in corre-spondence to meal times and portions. To go to the bathroom once a day should at least be a minimum to all, with the ex-ception of infants. During breastfeeding and bottle-feeding, occurrence in movements can range from several times a day to once a week.

Regarding the effects of touch on the bowel function there are many positive experiences. Regular abdominal massage can stop long-term constipation and should be tried before using laxatives, enemas or "plucking." In difficult cases one might need to massage the abdomen up to three times a day in the beginning in order to get the intestinal activity stimu-lated. For those testing abdominal massage for constipation purposes, it is guaranteed to start the bowls moving. It is in nature's interest to take care of all physical functions if it is only allowed to. Touch stimulates the parasympathetic ner-vous system assuring that visits to the "potty" may not be too rare!

Increased salivation

The majority of us who have tried to hold a speech or a presentation in front of a large group of people, know how the mouth in a stressful situation can turn into something that feels like an arid desert. The tongue literally sticks to the roof of the mouth, and without the blessed glass of water that some foreseeing person has put there, it might be hard to get the words out. Stress decreases the saliva in the oral cavity causing a dry mouth (xerostomia). If occurrence is infrequent no harm is done, but if xerostomia remains over a longer period of time, both teeth and digestion may suffer. If you are stressed and have a dry mouth there are good reasons to search for advice.

Saliva increases due to activity in the parasympathetic ner-vous system. Normally one liter of saliva is produced daily. Among its functions, saliva lubricates food for greater ease of swallowing and it also facilitates speaking. Furthermore, there are substances in saliva which stimulate the digestion of starch. Dental health is improved, aside from the intake of nutritional food and overall good dental hygiene, by sufficient saliva in the mouth. Therefore, you can, even though it might sound strange, massage to prevent dental cavities.

Increased concentration and smarter children

Observers of children have found that children's concentration ability improves after massage. In some way touch seems to coordinate the brain's flow of impulses creating order and efficiency in the system. In a study performed on adults in a workplace setting, the test subjects showed increased speed and accuracy in math computations after massage. The conclusion was made that touch increases concentration.

Claiming that children become smarter from touch might seem controversial. Nevertheless, in the last decades neurophysiologists have been able to prove that the chemistry, function, and structure of the brain is increased by rich stimulation. The tactile senses are represented in a large area of projection in the brain, therefore touching activates considerable parts of it. Brain exercises, in the form of tactile stimulation, seem to help children access their inherent intelligence in the most optimal way.

Touch and tactile experiences also create a state of calmness and security, which are prerequisites to learning. Tactile stimulation effects the ability of the brain to process impressions and learning, which the child experiences through real events, and which is done through the tactile sense. One can therefore say that touching your child means feeding its brain with nutritional food.

Appendix 1

Colic Massage

Colic can make a baby–and its parents–miserable for months. Classically, colic is characterized by the "rule of threes." The colic is expressed at least three hours a day, occurs at least three days a week and lasts three weeks to three months. Usually, the onset is about the age of three weeks.

The baby's crying often becomes harder and edgier as colic kicks in. You can tell the baby is miserable as it is inconsolable. It shows physical agitation by pulling the knees up to the abdomen, and crumbling up.

Up to 20 percent of all infants in the United States will be colicky whereas it is unheard of in most developing countries. The cause of infant colic is still a matter of debate among experts in the field. One fact physicians do seem to agree on is that infant colic and intestinal gas is painful for the baby. The situation is usually also very frustrating to the parents who powerlessly have to watch their baby in obvious pain.

Massage has proven to ease light gas problems to full blown colic. It stimulates the gastric-intestinal tract to function better. Parallel to daily massages it is suggested to carry the baby and to check the diet of the breastfeeding mother. Gas forming foods should be avoided and cow's milk, soy and fish can be expelled from the diet to see if that can help cure the ailing baby.

According to traditional Chinese medicine infant colic is often due to cold in the stomach. The above mentioned food is, in oriental medicine, considered cold in quality. Too much of this food creates energy stagnation with stabbing pain as a result. Therefore, it makes sense to keep the baby warm at all times. Hold it close and make sure its tummy is well covered. The breastfeeding mother could also eat ginger and other warming herbs to further add to the warming of the infant's stomach.

Colic massage is preferably done on a regular basis–at least once a day. In times of severe colic the massage can be applied up to three times a day. It might not be possible to find a perfect time to perform the massage since the baby might be more or less fussy all the time. Avoid massaging directly after the baby is fed however.

It is said that colic massage is the only massage allowed to be done with the baby crying. Even though it breaks your heart to hear your baby crying it is better to do the massage than not doing it at all.

The routine is simple and short, yet efficient enough to help the baby to pass gas. This is what you do:

Undress the baby from the belly down. Explain to it what you are going to do. Then take the pre-warmed oil and rub it in your palms. Start doing the colic massage routine.

"The Waterwheel"

Do alternating strokes from the upper abdomen and down. Scoop with your hands six times. (See J under Baby Massage – Chest & Abdomen).

"Sun and Moon"

Circle clockwise around the navel. One hand is making a full circle (sun) and the other hand does half a circle (moon). Repeat six times. (See H under Baby Massage – Chest & Abdomen).

"Knees to Stomach"

See Z under Baby Massage - Stretching. Repeat these three steps three times.

My nephew Vincent was colicky and on the day of his baptism he was not in a good mood. My sister asked me to massage his stomach before the ceremony took place in their home. As I did so we were both startled. When I did the "knees up" he loudly passed so much air we could not believe it. How such a tiny body as his (three months old) could hold that much air was a mystery to us. No wonder he was in pain!

Now Vincent is soon one year old and his colicky days are long gone. He grew out of it, as will most children. If the baby is bottled-fed and is long suffering from stomach pain and gas, it needs to be checked for allergies or food sensitivity.

Establish tranquil and reliable routines, be constant with bed and bath time and the baby may be reassured. Remember to treat yourself to a massage once in awhile, too. The calmer you are the safer the baby will feel. Parents may take turns attaching the baby to their bodies providing it with all the tactile nourishment and warmth necessary. Soon the colic will subside and you will all have made it through the tough time.

Appendix 2

Buddy Massage in Pre-School and School

To anyone with a special interest in the application of Child Massage and Buddy Massage in day care settings, pre-schools, schools etc., this appendix will offer you something to work with. I am aware of the present negativity connected to the act of touching children, especially in the U.S.A. This anti-tactile development is most sad and indicates how off the track society has gone. It is from touch deprivation and lack of emotional support that violence, criminality, and gang formations grow. Those with the calling to work with children often end up with the responsibility of solving these problems. To be aware and alert to catch a child in the risk zone of becoming a "problem" is not always easy. The sooner measures are taken to deter the tendency the better, of course. To find tools, which prevent problems and give opportunities to create a stable and improved basis for children to grow from, can be most inspiring. Massage can prove to be one of these tools. All the pre-school teachers and school teachers that I have talked to in Sweden who have tried massage, claim that it is the best thing they have ever done. In a kindergarten I visited recently, they have been incorporating massage in their activities on a daily basis for over five years already. They claim they would never go back to the old way of working again.

I realize the public needs to be educated and massage has to be freed from any indecency and ambiguity associated with it. With an explosion of sex infiltrating films, music videos, and commercials giving subtle suggestions to human interactions, a reaction of some kind has to be expected. On one hand, we see the poor skills of human tactile contact. The scale ranges from no contact at all to one of sexual advances. What has happened to all the tactile communication between these extremes? On the other hand, the focus on sexuality provokes some people to ban anything they think might be associated with it. Massage and touch techniques are such subjects, which often fall into this category.

I do not believe the world needs more insensitive, punishing or violent bodily contact. What I do believe in is motherly, fatherly, friendly, caring, empathetic, supporting touch which humans at any age can heal and grow from. So for you who ask from your heart to contribute to the peace in the world, here is theoretical and practical advice on how to apply Buddy Massage in pre-school and school.

Buddy Massage in Pre-School and School
When – Where – How

Buddy Massage is primarily meant to be a seated massage, which is easy to do in the classroom. Buddy Massage should be so simple that it is easily included in the school agenda without disturbing the curriculum.

When to do Buddy Massage

Buddy Massage is meant to fit into the ordinary school activity. The purpose behind it is that whenever the need occurs, massage can be adapted to fit in. When restlessness is increasing and concentration in the classroom is decreasing, the lesson can be interrupted for massage. After a moment of School Massage, the class is quiet again and the lesson can continue. Even a special time of the day can be set aside for massage breaks. Some prefer to start the school day with massage. Many times the morning tasks and transportation to school can be stressful. Starting the day with Buddy Massage can give both students and teachers the peace and quiet needed for teaching and inclination for studying.

Buddy Massage can also be done before the lunch break, if the break, of course, is not so late that everybody is starving! Massage before lunch creates better circumstances for a more peaceful atmosphere in the cafeteria and the body is prepared for better digestion.

Buddy Massage also can be added to the curriculum as a subject of its own or be done in combination with drama, sports or any other suitable subject.

To make transitions and schooling as smooth as possible it is useful to benefit from the effects of touch when children are starting school and changing to a new class or a new school with new classmates. First, the children are calmed and secondly, the bonding becomes stronger between students massaging each other. The unity is obvious in a class where the children have learned to take care of each other and touch each other in a friendly way.

When not to use Buddy Massage

As usual, the child itself must be willing to receive the massage. The child always decides over its own body when massage and touching are concerned. Buddy Massage should not be used for the purpose of healing injuries that have not first been examined by medical trained and licensed personnel.

Where to do Buddy Massage

Buddy Massage is easily done at the desks with the students sitting on their chairs. If a short massage routine is to be performed, massaging shoulders, neck and head, the student can sit as normal at their desks while the classmate stands behind them massaging. When a longer routine is done the student can turn the chair the other way and straddle it with the chest against the backrest. In this way, it is easier for the classmate to reach the back.

If there is room, the children can lie on the floor, too, on a sleeping pad for instance. When lying down the body tends to relax more, and deeper relaxation can be achieved. If the classroom is equipped with desks big enough to lie on the sleeping pads can be rolled out on them.

How Buddy Massage is taught to the children

For children in the lower grades, Buddy Massage can be introduced in the form of a fairy tale with massage techniques incorporated. The teacher tells the story while demonstrating the massage movements on a student, at the same time, one half of the class imitates the movements and the other half of the class receives. In upper grades, the seated massage can be taught in the same way. Begin with teaching one or a couple of massage movements and then later add a new movement with each massage time. Remember the way the teacher presents the activity gives the children the picture of what it is all about.

Stressing the sincerity and the importance of respect will teach the students to do the massage in a humble and loving way.

How to integrate touch in the teaching

Buddy Massage can become a positive instrument in the teaching of language. Words and vocals referring to body parts are pronounced at the same time as that particular body part is massaged. Memory is engaged through writing words with a finger on the thigh simultaneously as the word is spelled.

Incorporated in physical education, Buddy Massage can have a natural place as a relaxation exercise after sports. Here the students can take turns to massage each other as a positive round up to the end of the sports class.

Touch enhances body awareness and therefore massage can also be a component in drama exercises and body awareness training.

A few minutes of massage before a test or an exam can help students release unnecessary tension and increase concentration. Nervousness and performance anxiety may influence the results in a negative way. Through the calming effects of touch, the focus of the student turns to what he knows instead of what he does not know.

What to do with children with special needs

There might be mentally and/or physically handicapped

children with special needs in the school. In the chapter about Child Massage, it was discussed how to best meet the needs of these children. In schools for handicapped children and in ordinary schools where handicapped children are integrated, Child Massage can be used continuously. The best results are found if massage is given in addition to physical therapy or training sessions. Physical Therapists or assistants may be suited for the task.

Where handicapped children are integrated into a normal class, they should be treated as the other kids. They can participate in Buddy Massage with the rest of the class. If the handicapped child has an assistant, other massage techniques can naturally be performed if needed. For example, hand massage may be used to relax and loosen tensed, closed hands. Fine motor skills, like holding a pen, may function better if the sensory area of the brain is first activated through touch.

Children with late or unsatisfactory sensory integration are also school participants. (See the chapter on Sensory Integration). Indications may not have emerged earlier but they can surface when the child is expected to sit still at a desk and follow instructions. These children should receive support from both school personnel and family. Massage may be added as part of the recommended action program. Depending on how severe the problems are, a remedial teacher might need to help.

How to inform the parents about Buddy Massage

Although Buddy Massage principally is done with clothes on, it might be worthwhile informing the parents about the massage activities at school. There may be parents that object, on behalf of their children, to such intimate contact. Buddy Massage can be objectively presented in a newsletter or in an oral presentation at a parent-teacher association meeting. It is beneficial to be prepared and to have the purpose and the goal of the activity clear in one's mind. When it comes to tactile education in school, most parents react positively to massage and relaxation being taught at school. Learning to respect one's fellow human beings, and having the skill to comfort and calm a friend, is knowledge easily shared.

How to prepare for Buddy Massage

No practical preparation is needed for Buddy Massage. There should be no fuss when taking a break for five or ten minutes. The only thing the students must do before starting the activity is to ask permission to do the massage. Apart from that nothing special is demanded.

If a tape recorder is available, it might be a good idea to play some relaxing music. The right kind of music can create a peaceful and harmonious atmosphere in the classroom.

Good Luck!

Bibliography

Auckett A., Field T. *Baby Massage*. 1981

Auckett A. *Baby Massage: Parent-Child Bonding Through Touch*. 1989

Autton N. *Touch – An Exploration*. Longmann and Todd Ltd, 1989.

Ayres J. *Sensory Integration And The Child*. Western Psychological Services, 1979.

Babeshoff K. *Nurturing Touch: Instruction in the Art of Infant Massage*. Family Development Resources, 1993.

Brown C.C. *The Many Facets Of Touch*. The Foundation Of Experience: Its Importance Through Life, With Initial Emphasis For Infants And Young Children. Johnson & Johnson Baby Products Company pediatric round table series; 10, 1984.

Cohen S. *The Magic Of Touch: Revolutionary Ways To Use Your Most Powerful Sense*. Harper Collins, 1987.

Colton H. *The Gift Of Touch: How Physical Contact Improves Communication, Pleasure And Health*. Kensington Pub. Corporation. 1996

Field T. *Advances in touch. New Implications In Human Development*. Johnson & Johnson Consumer Products Inc., 1989.

Field T. *Touch*. MIT Press, 2003

Field T. *Infancy. The Developing Child*. Harvard University Press, 1990.

Field T. *Massage Reduces Anxiety In Child And Adolescent Psychiatric Patients*. Journal of American Academy of Child and Adolescent Psychiatry, January, 1992.

Field T. *Massage Therapy For Infants And Children*. Journal of Developmental and Behavioural Pediatrics, April 1995.

Field T. *Touch in Early Development*. Lawrence Erlbaum Assoc. 1995.

and Brain Development From Birth To Adolescence. Main Street Books, 1994.

Leboyer F. *Loving Hands: The Traditional Art Of Baby Massage.* Newmarket Press, 1997.

Liedloff J. *The Continuum Concept. Allowing Human Nature To Work Successfully.* Addison-Wesley Publishing Company, Inc., 1991

Maxwell-Hudson C. *The complete Book of Massage.* Random House Trade Paperback, 1988.

McClure V. S. *Infant Massage: A Handbook For Loving Parents.* Bantam Books, 1989.

Montagu A. *Touching: The Human Significance Of The Skin.* 3rd Edition. Harper & Row, Publishers, 1986.

Morris D. *The Naked Ape: A Zoologist's Study Of The Human Animal.* Dell Publishing Company, 1999.

Salter J. *The Incarnating Child.* Antroposophic Press, 1990.

Touch Points. Touch research abstracts. Touch Research Institute, Univeristy of Miami School of Medicine.

Thevenin T. *The Family Bed- An Age Old Concept In Child Rearing.* Perigee, 1987.

Uvnäs-Moberg K. *Oxytocin And Behaviour.* Annals of Medicine, October, 1994.

Uvnäs-Moberg K. *Physiological And Endocrine Effects Of Social Contact.* Institution for Physiology and Pharmacology, Karolinska Institute, Solna, Sweden, 1997.

Verny T. *The Secrets Of The Unborn Child.* Delta, 1994.

Walker P. *The Book Of Baby Massage: For A Happier, Healthier Child.* Kensington Pub. Corporation, 1998.

Walker P. Baby *Massage: A Practical Guide To Massage And Movement For Babies And Infants.* St. Martin's Press, 1996.

ACKNOWLEDGEMENTS

In the process of making this book I have been blessed by support from many great people. My dear husband Anders was behind me a 100% all the way. He also contributed with the beautiful photographs without which the book would have been naked. I thank him with all my heart.

Carolina Thorell, LenaMaria Brunhoff and Åsa Lundell helped me believe I could do this. I value their friendship forever.

I thank Annika Kjellgren, Kristina Eliaeson and my sister Anna Kengo for graciously "lending" me their children for models. These wonderful children are reflections of their parents' inner beauty.

I am so grateful to my son Sam and his friend Henrik for their contribution to the Buddy Massage section. They will always be in my heart.

My dear parents-in-law, Helion and Ulla-Britt Jelvéus, must be remembered for their help with the initial script. I also thank them for their support.

Lena Austin and Ylva Ellneby led me to the Swedish publisher for which I cannot thank them enough. Sweden was ready for this book, and it was the first of its kind, thanks to everybody at Utbildningsradions Förlag.

Bo Edelstam M.D did the medical review of the Swedish edition and gave valuable comments. I greatly appreciate his cooperation.

Victoria Ware took time out of her busy life to edit the English translation. For her extraordinary work and contribution I am forever indebted.

I thank David Shapiro, and Charlotte EinarsonTaylor for input and feedback on the English edition. I also thank Maria Grove at Touch Therapy Institute for never giving up hope on the English version of this book.

Loren Pollard of "Proof Positive," Americanized the grammar, spelling, and punctuation of this English edition. I am very grateful for your expertise.

Alan Chamberlain did a superb job on the cover layout and Brian Vatcher made the perfect finishing touches. Thank you guys!

Last, but not least, I want to humbly thank my parents Myrtel and Rainer Nyholm in Finland. The older I become the more I see their wisdom in child rearing. Their compassionate hearts will be my leading star for the rest of my life.

And to all not mentioned but not forgotten- love and light!

Lena Jelvéus

Index

Resources

A Foundation for Healthy Family Living
www.healthyfamily.com
Kalena Babeshoff
P.O. Box 1665
Sonoma, CA 95476
Phone: 707- 996.3545
Fax: 707- 996.7187
E-mail: info@healthyfamily.org
Providing educational materials that enhance respectful communication and nurturing touch.
Infant Massage training, educational programs and early intervention agency training.

International Association of Infant Massage
www.iaim-us.com
1891 Goodyear Avenue, Suite 622
Ventura, CA 93003
Phone: 805-644-8524
Fax: 805-644-7699
E-mail: IAIM4US@aol.com
The mission of the International Association of Infant Massage (IAIM®) is to promote nurturing touch and communication through training, education, and research so that parents, caregivers, and children are loved, valued, and respected throughout the world community.
IAIM® trains and certifies Certified Infant Massage Instructors (CIMI®) who in turn teach parents and caregivers to massage their babies.

Swedish Health Institute®
www.swedishhealthinstitute.com
17525 Ventura Blvd. #108
Encino, CA 91316
Phone: 818-817-0049, 818-730-5200
Fax: 818-817-0958
E-mail: info@swedishhealthinstitute.com
The author of this book, Lena Jelveus, conducts classes in Child Massage for parents, caretakers and massage therapists. Private instuctions for parents and families also available.